Tastemaker Records

Executive Producers Club

Tastemaker Records

Executive Producers Club

The Gothenburg Mix

Matthew Cepican

Musician, Original Music Composer, Paralegal

Tastemaker Records Executive Producers Club the

The Gothenburg Mix © 2022 all rights reserved

Matthew Cepican © all rights reserved

9 781387 649938

Tastemaker Records Executive Producers Club

Publishing © 2022 all rights reserved

Because of the dynamic nature of the Internet, any address or links contained in the book might have changed since publication.

ISBN: 978-1-387-64993-8 (sc)

Table of Contents

Introduction

Chapter I   Cabinet Positions

Chapter II   Live Music Element

Chapter III   Thespian Element

Chapter IV   Health and Wellness Element

Chapter V   International Film Festival Element

Chapter VI   International Tastemaker Fest
                Theme Song

Chapter VII   The War on Poverty

Chapter VIII   The Cycle of Poverty In Film

Chapter IX   Intelligently Designing New
                Complex Systems

Chapter X   Peer Pressure Problems with
                Urban & Regional Planning

Chapter XI   Public School Funding Models

Chapter XII   Urban Revitalization and
                Redevelopment

Chapter XIII   Social Movement Effects and
                Complex System Designs

Chapter XIV   Employing Unrealized Potential
                from Inefficient Conglomeration

Chapter XV   Ill Effects of Modern Social Safety Net
                Programs

Chapter XVI   Planning Future Communities with the
                Changing of Ineffective Social Safety Net
                Programs

Chapter XVII   IQCF Articles of Incorporation

Chapter XVIII IQCF Bylaws

Chapter XIX   Conflict-of-Interest Policy and Agreement

Chapter XX   The IQCF Mission

Chapter XXI   Articles of Incorporation Acknowledgement

Chapter XXII   EIN [Employer Identification Number]

Chapter XXIII   The IRS 1023 Document

Chapter XXIV   The Grants Mosaic 2022

Chapter XXV   IQCF [DEI] Research 2023

Chapter XXVI   Diversity, Cultural Equity & Inclusion 2022

Chapter XXVII   The IQCF 2023

Chapter XXVIII   New Films & Venues

Chapter XXIX   War on Poverty Changes

Chapter XXX   Sustainability Research 2023

Chapter XXXI   Talent Attraction & Ambition

Chapter XXXII   Planning IQCF 2024

Chapter XXXIII   Glossary

Introduction

The Gothenburg Mix is the synthesis of *the International Tastemaker Fest Thesis, the International Quint Cities Festival,* and *the IQCF 2023* publishings. *The Gothenburg Mix* combines the previous publishings and helps our readers see the new, modern complex systems we are developing. The IQCF mission involves developing new, modern complex systems that end the wealth gap, cycle of poverty and systemic racism, both real and perceived. *The Gothenburg Mix* represents the changes we are seeing since the original publishing of *the International Tastemaker Fest Thesis.*

The Executive Producers Club established the new IQCF nonprofit corporation in 2020. *The International Quint Cities Festival* is the result of diligent research and modern urban & regional planning practices. We are building on the lessons learned from observing other nonprofit corporations in the QC region. We believe you will see the progress as you read the EPC publishings.

Chapter I we will review and welcome our new Executive Producers Club Cabinet members 2022/2023. The new Cabinet is a mix of promotions and new members who obtained the votes. We believe you will enjoy the new members of the Cabinet with the rest of the EPC Cabinet alumni.

Chapter II we will review the international music venues we are developing including our new international town of Glasgow, Scotland. Every year we are developing a new international town that will join our international festival. Someday, the IQCF will be in every international town on the same day. The idea is complex, and we are helping develop the new world systems that end the wealth gap, cycle of poverty and systemic racism.

Chapter III we will review the thespian element of the IQCF. We must research the thespian element because the Greek named Thespis was the first stage star of western civilization. The Super Bowl, Las Vegas, Lollapalooza, etc. can all give the Greek Thespis thanks regarding building stages with characters and entertaining the masses.

Chapter IV we will review the Health &
Wellness element of the IQCF. Health & Wellness
is becoming a regular part of modern humankind.
We believe the Health & Wellness element of the
IQCF will become developed and might become a
new nonprofit corporation.

The international film festival element of the
IQCF is diligently curated from every international
film festival. The IQCF volunteers research every
film festival and decide what films we want on the
IQCF film festival roster. Chapter V will review
the new films who joined the IQCF film festival
roster this year. We believe the films on our IQCF
film list help build our region and teach
multicultural lessons.

Chapter VI reviews the IQCF theme song.
Originally composed with the publishing of *the
International Tastemaker Fest Thesis,* the IQCF
theme song is a new world theme song. We believe
musicians of every nation will hear the ideas and
join the orchestra. Someday, maybe a musician will
compose the lyrics.

The War on Poverty is always changing.
Chapter VII will review the original ideas from the

War on Poverty chapter from *the International Quint Cities Festival.* You will see lots of revises and language changes from the original War on Poverty chapter in *the International Tastemaker Fest Thesis* because we are researching and developing lots of new language being when describing the wealth gap, cycle of poverty and systemic racism. We are building on the original War on Poverty chapter with new emerging diversity, cultural equity and inclusion scholarly research being published since 2020.

Chapter VIII will review the theories we developed regarding the cycle of poverty in film. You will see new language building on the original observations of the cycle of poverty in film. We are identifying the origins of the wealth gap, cycle of poverty and systemic racism in our nation. Employing examples from the stereotypes of the cycle of poverty we see in film helps us get at the root of the origin of the wealth gap, cycle of poverty and systemic racism.

Intelligently designing new, modern complex systems is the task we are pursuing. Chapter IX is the foundation of the theories upon which we are building. The synthesis of these publishings matters because we are getting at the origins of the wealth gap. Understanding the origins of the wealth gap is a challenge. We believe you will understand how the wealth gap was an effect of the 14th Amendment era lawmakers when you finish *the Gothenburg Mix*.

Peer pressure problems with urban & regional planning is a fact. Chapter X will review the ways in which peer pressure causes planning challenges. Conformity peer pressure is a cause of some of the cross-class, cross-cultural conflicts in some neighborhoods. However, we are embracing the emerging multiethnic audience in our nation. Someday soon our national population will be a multiethnic majority and we will be prepared. These publishings will help urban & regional planners develop premier communities with our new multiethnic majority audiences.

Chapter XI is the start of our public school funding models research. *The Gothenburg Mix* employs the public school funding models of our nation when getting at the root of the wealth gap, cycle of poverty and systemic racism.

Understanding how public school funding is a clue regarding the wealth gap requires diligent historical research and undivided attention while reading. Public school funding models are mentioned in several chapters because that is a serious clue regarding the origins of the modern wealth gap.

Urban revitalization & redevelopment is occurring in the QC because of URTEs [urban renewal tax exemptions]. Chapter XII will examine the URTE zones of Davenport specifically. URTEs are a cool urban & regional planning approach. URTE zones are full of urban blight. Boards on windows and doors, etc. Property owners are hesitant in raising the assessed value of the property because that will raise the property taxes. However, with the new URTE laws codified, if you raise the property value of a property in an identified URTE zone, then the property owner is exempt from 10 years of property taxes. We will review the URTE zones in Davenport specifically.

Chapter XIII researches the connection between social movement effects and complex system designs. Are social movements the most effective means of changing the status quo? We answer the tough questions. Education of interested parties can affect change from within the system. The masses like a big party, but social movements often end in quagmires of unrealized potential. We believe change can occur with similar minds solving the same social problems more efficiently in the civic arena rather than hastily organized movements with vague direction.

Employing unrealized potential from inefficient conglomeration is the natural result of researching ineffective social movements. Chapter XIV reviews agglomeration and conglomeration in terms of masses of people assembled at a single place and why that is inefficient conglomeration of resources regarding affecting social change. If you provide the masses with problem solving skills in public school, then social unrest rarely occurs. However, we are learning that public school funding models are shortchanging our marginalized populations.

Ill effects of modern, social safety net programs are the subject of Chapter XV. Our nation must maintain a minimum social safety net. We are the wealthiest nation on Earth. However, we ask the question "Are modern social safety net programs ending the wealth gap, cycle of poverty and systemic racism?" If not, then should we design new social safety net programs?

Chapter XVI researches the idea of planning future communities with the changing of inefficient social safety net programs. We must maintain social safety net programs. However, we can and must design social safety net programs that help end the wealth gap, cycle of poverty and systemic racism. We researched the debate regarding the effect social safety net programs regarding the widening wealth gap, cycle of poverty and systemic racism. If social safety net programs enable the cycle of poverty, then what is the answer? Public school funding models. Public school funding models are the relic of 14th Amendment era lawmakers and the origin of the modern wealth gap, cycle of poverty and systemic racism. Changing the way we fund our public schools is a sign that the origins of the modern wealth gap, cycle of poverty and systemic racism are being acknowledged. New law changes elsewhere will follow.

Chapters XVII through XXIII are the IQCF articles of incorporation documents. We encourage you research our incorporation documents, especially if you are developing a nonprofit corporation. The legalese is somewhat difficult if you are unfamiliar with the legal profession language. However, that is why our articles of incorporation documents are herein because you can research and employ similar language if you are developing a nonprofit corporation.

The IQCF articles of incorporation is the document we entered at the Iowa Secretary of State. The Iowa Secretary of State received the IQCF articles of incorporation and mailed us an acknowledgement letter that the IQCF is incorporated in the State of Iowa. However, obtaining the corporation acknowledgement letter from the Iowa Secretary of State isn't the letter that declares a corporation is tax-exempt in the eyes of the Internal Revenue Service.

Obtaining tax-exempt status from the Internal Revenue Service requires several other documents including the IQCF mission, Bylaws [including anti-discrimination policy], EIN [employer identification number and Conflicts-of-Interest policy. All these documents must be present when you enter the IRS 1023. That means you must upload all these documents online at www.pay.gov when you enter the IRS 1023. The IRS will then review the 1023 application with all the supporting documents and after several months will mail you the IRS "Letter of Determination" that states the corporation is a nonprofit tax-exempt organization in the eyes of the Internal Revenue Service. Grant applications require applicants are tax-exempt organizations, otherwise, you are ineligible regarding grant funding.

Chapter XX is the examination of the IQCF nonprofit mission. Every nonprofit corporation must develop a mission. The IRS 1023 and annual 990 must contain the nonprofit mission statement. Chapter X provides an in-depth review of the IQCF nonprofit mission. The IQCF mission is developing a diverse, inclusive Quint Cities region with an emphasis on cultural equity. Every nonprofit corporation revises their mission here and there, and the purpose of publishing our mission is because we might make subtle changes after a while.

Chapter XXIV covers the 2022 grants mosaic. We employ the term "grants mosaic" because we must view all the grant recipients as one giant mosaic of nonprofit groups in the QC region. We encourage you review the 2022 grant recipients. We will publish the new list of local grant recipients every year because learning who receives what and how much will help other nonprofit groups develop successful grant proposals.

Every grant application asks specific questions. Every grant application is similar; however, every grant application contains unique questions that are specific of that foundation or grant making organization. Regardless of the foundation or grant making organization, we encourage you research the grant mosaic list we compiled. Researching the local grants mosaic will help you with grant applications because you can see what kind of grant requests are being funded. The IQCF volunteers research the grants mosaic every cycle because we request similar grant funding that other arts & culture nonprofit groups request and receive.

The IQCF volunteers diligently research talents who come through town from other regions of our nation and international towns. Chapter XXV reviews all the new talents we observed in our local venues in 2022. We encourage you research all the artists, purchase the music, merch, tickets and join the mailing list. We want these talents coming here every year because that helps us build the QC region as a destination like Nashville.

Diversity, cultural equity, and inclusion are modern ways in which we are developing new complex systems. Chapter XXVI is an in-depth observation of how diversity, cultural equity, and inclusion can identify the origins of the modern wealth gap, cycle of poverty and/or systemic racism both real and perceived. Changing inefficient complex systems is hard and we must learn the origins of inefficient complex systems first.

Chapter XXVII is the preview of the IQCF 2023. We synthesize all the lessons from the inaugural IQCF 2022 and build on the successes. The inaugural IQCF food drive was a smashing success and the thank you letter from the Community Center Circle Food Pantry is encouragement that gives the IQCF volunteers a sense of accomplishment. The IQCF is an arts & culture festival, however, our mission is helping our low-income, underserved, marginalized populations develop a sense of belonging and community building.

The new films and venues we researched are building our international plan. The original idea of developing a new international town each year is from *the International Tastemaker Fest Thesis.* Chapter XXVIII is the list of new films, and films we raised from past years. The new international town is Glasgow, Scotland. We encourage you view the films and research the new international IQCF town.

The War on Poverty is always changing. Chapter XXIX reviews the changing war on poverty after researching the efficacy of our nations' social safety net programs. Further, we ask the question; "Are social safety net programs ending the wealth gap, cycle of poverty and/or systemic racism?" These are the tough questions we answer herein.

Chapter XXX reviews the modern ideas of cultural sustainability. Environmental preservation and cultural sustainability are connected with the theme of the wealth gap, cycle of poverty and systemic racism. We must research all these ideas when developing new, modern complex systems that end the wealth gap, cycle of poverty and systemic racism.

Talent attraction and ambition are regular themes here in the QC region. QC town planners are always designing plans that will attraction talent and retain talent. Further, groups like the QC Chamber are always developing ideas on how we can retain our local talents in the QC. Chapter XXXI builds on these ideas and we believe we developed some good plans regarding talent attraction and retention.

Chapter XXXII is the IQCF 2023 planning ideas. We learned a lot from the inaugural IQCF 2022, and we are building on the best ideas and successes. We encourage you review the IQCF 2023 plans and contact the IQCF volunteers with ideas, suggestions and/or questions. The IQCF volunteers are the best feedback. We will see you at the festival. Thank you.

Chapter I

Cabinet Positions

"The design of the Executive Producers
Club espouses the world systems of democracy and
capitalism/free enterprise. We encourage you
design and copy the Executive Producers Club
when developing whatever dreams you desire. Our
Executive Producers' Club are merely and arts &
culture nonprofit organization and urban & regional
planners developing a system through which we
accomplish complex tasks. Every start up business
must develop a business plan with clear objectives
and an organizational design that ensures
partnerships and collaborations. The Executive
Producers' Club is the business plan, and the

objective is building the... *International Quint Cities Festival [IQCF]* mission.

The IQCF mission is developing naturally every year. Building on the research, experiences, and feedback of our IQCF volunteers is a key regarding changing the inefficient complex systems that cause barriers and prevent individuals from obtaining access of resources. The access that should be here is hindered because of inefficient urban & regional planning and that is a problem we can change. However, diligent research must occur first.

The first annual IQCF inaugural food drive was a success. The IQCF volunteers understand why food insecurity and housing instability is the result of unequal access of resources. Food insecurity and housing instability aren't the cause of social problems, but rather the result inefficient complex systems. The debate regarding inefficient complex systems that cause the wealth gap, cycle of poverty and systemic racism is huge. Why are some complex systems designed inefficiently and cause the wealth gap, cycle of poverty and systemic racism? These are the tough questions we will answer herein. The task is large and the IQCF volunteers are on a mission.

Executive Producers Club Cabinet
Positions effective December 21st, 2022

President

Crystal St. Germaine obtained the votes and will become President of the Executive Producers Club effective December 21st, 2022, until December 21st, 2023. Responsibilities include developing interpersonal connections with the Quad Cities Chamber of Commerce, local music venues and musicians.

Vice President

Karen Blomme obtained the votes and will become Vice President of the Executive Producers Club effective December 21st, 2022, until December 21st, 2023. Responsibilities include developing interpersonal connections with the Dublin, Ireland Chamber of Commerce, local music venues and musicians.

Treasurer

Jenna Morehouse obtained the votes and will become Treasurer of the Executive Producers Club effective December 21st, 2022, until December

21st, 2023. Responsibilities include developing interpersonal connections with the Hamburg, Germany Chamber of Commerce, local music venues and musicians and the Quad Cities Chamber of Commerce, local music venues, musicians, museums, and art galleries.

Secretary

Brian Saude obtained the votes and will become Secretary of the Executive Producers Club effective December 21st, 2022, until December 21st, 2023. Responsibilities include developing interpersonal connections with the Hamburg, Germany Chamber of Commerce, local music venues and musicians.

International Film/Television Sync License Executive

Angela Meyer obtained the votes and will become International Film/Television Sync License Executive of the Executive Producers' Club effective December 21st, 2022, until December 21st, 2023. Responsibilities included developing interpersonal connections with international film festivals and the music sync license personnel.

Director of Personnel

Ricci St. Germaine obtained the votes and will become Director of Personnel of the Executive Producers Club effective December 21st, 2022, until December 21st, 2023. Responsibilities include developing interpersonal connections with musicians in the Quad Cities, Dublin, Ireland, Hamburg, Germany, Barcelona, Spain, London, England and Reykjavik, Iceland.

International Musicians Executive

Travis Barker obtained the votes and will become International Musicians Executive of the Executive Producers Club effective December 21st, 2022, until December 21st, 2023. Responsibilities include developing interpersonal connections with the Barcelona, Spain Chamber of Commerce, local music venues and musicians.

Sergeant at Arms

MCLogo☆ obtained the votes and will become Sergeant at Arms of the Executive

Producers Club effective December 21st, 2022, until December 21st, 2023. Responsibilities include developing interpersonal connections with the London, England Chamber of Commerce, local music venues and musicians.

Chapter II

Live Music Element

Live music is the initial inspiration of *the International Quint Cities Festival.* Music festivals are moments when humanity becomes one will with unified purpose. Designing *the international Quint Cities Festival* became multivenue, multithemed, multimedia and multitown on the international stage. The Executive Producers Club research the music venues in each international town and then develops the venues. *The International Quint Cities Festival* alumnus talent can then perform in the international venues during each year between *the International Quint Cities Festival* on the last Saturday of July every year. I developed this plan after reading and hearing bands experiences with performing in venues overseas. The venues on *the International Quint Cities Festival* are being developed in the similar fashion bands are developed. Yes, artist and venue development are real.

Musicians must learn music venues survive when the most bands end live performances after a few years. Thus, the music venues become like the proverbial "5th" Beatle and the venue stage becomes a "member" of the band. The venue stages are magical treasure deserving as much respect as the bands performing on the venue stages. The other element of employing the multivenue model is the equal distribution of festival revenue in the Quad Cities and every international town we develop. Large festivals with one large stage and a huge crowd are fun. The multivenue design of *the International Tastemaker Fest* develops a festival scene all the international towns enjoy rather that one central site. Becoming a new international town on *the International Quint Cities Festival* are really cool because you are joining the club.

Live Music Element

The Redstone Room Davenport, IA

https://www.rivermusicexperience.org

RIBCO Rock Island, IL

https://www.ribco.com

The Rust Belt East Moline, IL

www.therustbeltqc.com

Rozztox Rock Island, IL

www.rozztox.com

Codfisth Hollow Maquoketa, IA

www.codfishhollowbarnstormers.com

Sala Apolo Barcelona, Spain

www.sala-apolo.com

Sala Razzmatazz Barcelona, Spain

www.salarazzmatazz.com

Tax Slayer Center Moline, IL

www.taxslayercenter.com

Whelans Dublin, Ireland

www.whelanslive.com

Logo Hamburg, Germany

www.logohamburg.de

Mojo Hamburg, Germany

www.mojo.de

Roundhouse, London, England

www.roundhouse.org.uk

The Garage, Glasgow, Scotland

Chapter III

Thespian Element

The thespian element of *the International Tastemaker Fest* teaches us all the value of learning the origin of "the stage." The earliest civilized tribes built theatre stages and entertained each other. The thespian element reminds us of why the stage matters. "...Archaeologists from ancient Rome and Greece believe *Thespis* was the first ever person...playing a character on a stage...and the derivation of the name *Thespis* is our modern term "thespian."[i] Several sources argue he was the first touring artist performing in several towns and hauling his scenes, costumes, music instruments in his cart. *Thespis* was a singer of dithyrambs, or songs of mythology with verses and chorus.[ii] Thus, *Thespis* was the first modern rock star of Western

Civilization. We are certain every culture contains similar characters like *Thespis.*

Personally, when I was a freshman in Bettendorf High School, I was the drummer in the *Kit Kat Club* band in the musical production of *Cabaret.* My girlfriend was a *Kit Kat Club* dancer in the musical and that is why we became an item. I attended her senior prom with her when I was a freshman. The *Cabaret* experience is when I really learned stage skills, lighting, stage cues, and the like. High School theatre and rock concerts are similar because the stage. Bands touring must remember the experiences of *Thespis* and the origin of "the stage" in Western Civilization. Other world cultures must research the similar characters who were the first stage performers of their respective regions. We will develop theatre stages in each of the international towns we develop in *the International Tastemaker Fest.*

Thespian Element

Adler Theatre Davenport, IA
www.adlertheatre.com

Circa '21 Rock Island, IL
www.circa21.com

Riverbank Dublin, Ireland
www.riverbank.ie

Chapter IV

Health and Wellness Element

       The Health and Wellness element of *the International Quint Cities Festival* is a moment when festival attendees can sample the newest and best health products. *The Bix 7* race promotes health and wellness and *SCW Pro Wrestling* is a local business encouraging the development of the physical body with elements of theatre and sports entertainment. Museums help develop our general sense of wellbeing through fine arts and culture and the *Kilkennys' Bix Fest* encourages the healthy interaction with festival attendees enjoying themselves and each other. The Health and Wellness element of *the International Tastemaker Fest* will evolve every year with *the International Tastemaker Fest*. We will develop museums and sports entertainment in each town of *the International Tastemaker Fest.*

You might wonder why Pro Wrestling, sports entertainment and museums are considered "health and wellness." We believe Pro Wrestling, sports entertainment and museums promote health and wellness because Pro Wrestling entails being in physical shape. The pro wrestling matches are pure theatre with dialogue, characters, masks, and other props. Museums are calm, quiet and make you question beliefs and help develop a sense of wellbeing you never experience in other venues. We will develop museums and other sports entertainment attractions within the health and wellness element of *the International Tastemaker Fest.* Kilkennys' *Bix Fest* embodies health and wellness because large crowds of people are all joined with similar purpose of enjoying a festival atmosphere. Festivals are one of the best activities and remind citizens of what makes us all similar with the shared experience of the large crowd of a festival.

Health and Wellness Venues

The Bix 7 Race Davenport, IA
www.bix7.com

Bix Museum Davenport, IA
www.bixmuseum.org

Kilkennys' Bix Fest Davenport, IA

SCW Pro Wrestling Davenport, IA
www.scw-pro.com

German American Heritage Center and Museum
www.gahc.org

Figge Art Museum
www.figgeartmuseum.org

Chapter V

International Film Festival Element

    The International Quint Cities Festival film element are the films we want shaping our perceptions and perspectives. The following films are in *the International Quint Cities Festival* film rotation. The Executive Producers Club will select films from the following list in Chapter V and develop the film festival element every year. The Executive Producers Club will select other films and the list will grow. The following films are merely the first films of the inaugural *International Tastemaker Fest*. We encourage you view each film in *the International Tastemaker Fest* film list and learn the lessons, characters, and production staffs. These are the individuals in the film industry with whom we are developing music sync license contracts between films and the musical talent at *the International Tastemaker Fest* every year.

The film industry is becoming one of the most influential change agents ever. Like the thespian element, the film element is an evolution of the concept of "the stage." The film industry presents productions in movie theatres, and this is the modern adaptation of theatre stages from antiquity and the dawn of civilization. The Executive Producers Club will develop the *Figge Art Museum, Rogalski Center,* and *Centennial Hall* as the main venues when present *the International Tastemaker Fest* films every year. We will develop other venues when *the International Tastemaker Fest* film element becomes well established. Remember the design of *the International Tastemaker Fest* is multivenue, multitheme and multimedia. We want the festival attendees roaming amongst all the Quad Cities and international towns' businesses involved with *the International Tastemaker Fest.*

International Film Festival Element

Adam
www.strandreleasing.com

Alex & Sylvia
www.brcweb.com

Aria
www.161films.com

Asymmetry
www.thisandthat.rs

Bangla
www.fandango.it

Battlescar
www.atlasv.io

Ben Hur
www.mgm.com

Beetlejuice
www.warnerbros.com/beetlejuice.com

Blade Runner
www.warnerbrothers.com

Chicuarotes
www.lacorrientedelgolfo.net

Crescendo
www.ccc-film.im-netz.de

Chryzinium
www.matchlightfilms.com

Compartments
www.compartments-film.com

Crush Hour
www.crushhourfilm.com

Crystal Swan
www.loco-films.com

Daughter
www.dariakashcheeva.com

Dragonfly Eyes
www.xubing.com

Fig Tree
www.lamasfilms.com

First Night Nerves
www.goldenscene.com

Frankie
www.osomeafuria.com

Haunt
www.beckwoods.com

Joy
www.abkco.com

Kayantar
www.imdb.com/title/tt10416128/

La Pequena Suiza
www.nadieesperfecto.com

Leaving Afghanistan
www.loco-films.com

Leeches
www.zillionfilm.com

Leona
www.menemshafilms.com

Les Miserables
www.srabfilms.fr

Lillian
www.cercamon.biz

Letters from War
www.osomeafuria.com

Marshmallows
www.imcine.gob.mx

Masters of Love
www.truckfilms.co.uk

Merry Chistmas, Yiwu
www.bocalupofilms.com

Metal Heart
www.bankside-films.com

Movements
www.jeongdahee.com

My Name is Sara
www.mynameissara.com

Night of the Babysitter
www.nightofthebabysitter.com

Obon
www.obonfilm.com

Orchid
Marit Stafstrom

Our Mother
www.perspectivefilms.fr

Parasite
www.cj.net

Paris Song
www.kazakhfilmstudios.kz

Persian Lessons
www.hypepro.tv

Piola
www.piolafilm.com

Proxima
www.dariusfilms.com

Relic
www.fiction.net.au

Salam
www.salaudmorisset.com

Seferad
www.sefaradmovie.com

Sibel
www.rivafilmde

Silence of the Sirens
www.dianavidrascu.com

Sobibor
www.samuelgoldwynfilms.com

Spring
www.festagent.com

Strangers' Reunion
www.sargentliz.com

Teen Spirit
www.bleeckerstreetmedia.com

Tel Aviv on Fire
www.cohenmedia.net

Tesla
www.passagepictures.com

The Awakening of the Ants
www.cinemaldito.com

The Cotton Wool War
www.imdb.com

The Cube Phantom
www.alamlaukinlun.wixsite.alanlau

The Day Grunge Died
www.skinandbonesfilm.com

The First Class
www.myungeunkim.com

The Mover
www.mistrusmedia.lv

The Planters
www.theplantersfilm.com

The Presence of the Dead
www.berlinale.de

Tully
www.focusfeatures.com

Volunteer
www.sulacofilm.ch

Worst Case, We Get Married
www.sevilleinternational.com

While At War
www.modmedia.es

Zana
www.crossingbridgesfilms.com

1945
www.katapultfilm.hu

Chapter VI

The International Quint Cities Festival Theme Song
[rough draft]

The International Quint Cities Festival
theme song compositional design is with an
orchestra in mind. The rough draft is merely the
recording that copyrights the name, image, likeness,
mechanical, nonmechanical, sync license, digital
distribution, and the publishing and performance
rights of the composition. When you hear the rough
draft of the composition, you must imagine an
orchestra full of strings and dancing. I personally
composed *the International Quint Cities Festival*
thesis imagining the entire world dancing with a
large orchestra. Months of thought of what *the
International Quint Cities Festival* theme song
should sound like is a complement. The truth is the

melody was developed in my mind in 2007. The melody and rhythm were a reoccurring theme I developed in my daydreams while practicing my immigration paralegal skills.

The melody of the composition is a way of expressing my thoughts on my teaching career. I am an ESL [English Second Language] teacher. All my students are English language learners. I was the only Caucasian in the room and almost all my students were Mexican Americans with a few whites, African Americans, Cambodians, and Pacific Islanders. South of Baseline in the Rialto High School zone is almost all Mexican American. North of Baseline in the Eisenhower High School zone is the majority African- American student population and further north on Riverside past Palm is the Carter High School zone and the highest Rialto property tax. I will teach property tax and public school funding models in Chapter 11.

"Anchor babies" is the term a lot of people employ because the majority of my students' parents are from Mexico. My students were born in the U.S. of parents that are Mexican citizens. If you look at the Rialto Middle School yearbook every year from 1977 until present, then you observe a large demographic shift researchers call "white flight." "…The Kerner Report …shamed white society…when fleeing…the cities…in exchange of suburban living, where...blacks...were...excluded from employment, housing, and educational opportunities. The reports' famous conclusion: "Our nation is...observing defacto...segregation..."[iii] The Colton/Rialto/Fontana region of the Inland Empire is considered suburban. This is why colleges and universities research the Colton/Rialto/Fontana region specifically. Southern California might be the most researched "urban sprawl" region of our nation.

Researching the Rialto Middle School yearbooks, you observe in the 1970s that 99 percent of all the students were white. When the large employer Kaiser Steel in Fontana closed their plant, urban & regional planners observed "white flight." The Rialto Middle School demographic shift from 1977 until present is researched in our colleges and universities as an example of "white flight." Almost every current Rialto Middle School student is of Mexican descent with a small percentage of whites, African American, Cambodians and Pacific Islanders. Most of the Cambodians in Rialto were originally refugees from Pol Pots' Khmer Rouge. The effects of "white flight" cause an interesting cultural mix in the Colton/Rialto/Fontana region being researched in our colleges and universities. The Colton/Rialto/Fontana region observes further divisions with the southern areas between Hwy 10 and

Baseline being majority Mexicans and the areas north of Baseline being majority African American. Far south of Rialto on Riverside Dr. and entering Riverside, CA, you see the demographics change because of the University of California Riverside.

Thus, change vs. continuity is the question in the Inland Empire cities like Colton, Rialto and Fontana. *The International Quint Cities Festival* is the change vs. continuity book the entire world must read. *The International Quint Cities Festival* is being designed with the *Executive Producers Club* and diversity, cultural equity and inclusion will be the result of clever urban & regional planning. The entire world will learn from the urban & regional planning of the Quad Cities and the Quad Cities will learn urban & regional planning ideas from the entire world. The design of *the International Quint Cities Festival* theme song composition encourages musicians from the entire world learn and perform the song with a large orchestra. *The International Quint Cities Festival* is an honest observation of our communities, nation and the world becoming diverse and developing urban & regional planning complex systems with the inclusion of marginalized segments of the population.

Like agglomeration in business, races somehow clump with each other, and racial and cultural diversity must occur naturally with clever urban & regional planning designs. We all like China Town, Korea Town, Little Mexico west of Chicago, etc. However, we must realize that the de facto segregation that occurs in every nation must be researched with diversity and inclusion in mind. Becoming a global citizen entails diligently researching several elements of diversity while at the same moment ending social friction caused when we try and force racial and cultural integration. *The International Quint Cities Festival* is a diversification plan employing what makes us all similar regardless of race and culture. Music, arts, theatre, and food are what make us all similar regardless of race and culture and *the International Quint Cities Festival* is the vehicle of developing truly global citizens.

Chapter VII

The War on Poverty

The war on poverty is ancient. The
moments and significance of LBJ's "War on
Poverty" are gone from modern memories. New
individuals researching urban & regional planning
complex systems are intelligently designing modern
complex systems aimed at ending the wealth gap,
cycle of poverty and systemic racism. Complex
systems are continually being refined and changed
with this aim in mind. A kinder, gentler society is
indeed within our reach. We will examine the
intriguing dynamics of complex systems, identify
perceived social problems, and design the best
urban & regional planning practices. The superior
system of democracy and free enterprise are themes
we will research with examples from the entire

world. The purpose of my theses is presenting research in an educational and intentionally entertaining manner. Edutainment, if you will. Making learning fun is cool. My sincere desire is you enjoy reading my thesis.

Ending the cycle of poverty is one of the main elements of the "American Dream." We advertised the American dream in Europe since the earliest moments of our nation. Gilberts Town [modern Bettendorf, Iowa] advertised in Europe the wonderful farm soil that can raise "…crops of all types…."[iv] The Quad Cities witnessed the arrival of thousands of German and Irish immigrants. The immigrants were experiencing the cycle of poverty when they arrived. We will examine the early German and Irish immigrant experience and apply the lessons in our modern community. New immigrants arrive in the Quad Cities every moment because we are the world model of the American dream. The German and Irish immigrants ended the cycle of poverty and became pillars of the Quad Cities, our nation, and the world. The famine in Ireland was the primary cause of the Irish immigration surge. The Quad Cities, like New

York, became an Irish American region. The Irish and Germans built the Quad Cities with blood, sweat and tears. The Irish immigrants fought the German immigrants because the language barrier and when our public schools codified English language instruction in our public schools, the fighting between Irish and German immigrants ended. Our modern Quad Cities immigrants from Vietnam and Mexico must understand and learn that the language barrier can cause social unrest. Thankfully, our public schools teach in English and speaking the same language is how we build a shared dream. E Pluribis Unum. Regarding speaking the English language, the English spoken in the Quad Cities is called "accent free" English and English language learners learn English best from "accent free" English. Cash crops and the Mississippi River is why we are all here, however, our "accent free" English is of value in all kinds of international business. Other nations learn English best from "accent free" English. We will identify the indigenous tribes of the Quad Cities region and detail the significant moments of Chief Blackhawks' agreements with the US government. The Quad

Cities African **American** experience is joined with the Blackhawk tribe through marriage. Genealogists are observing the mix of African **Americans** with the Blackhawk and other local tribes. The first house in Bettendorf was the dwelling of a man named Dred Scott. Scott County, Iowa is arguably the best county in Iowa. We will identify the other Iowa towns on the Underground Railroad like Stanton, Grinnell, Yetter, Parnell and Edgington in Illinois.

The first railroad bridge across the Mississippi River was built in Davenport and Westward expansion became realized in earnest. Who built that bridge? Local legend says Irish immigrants built that bridge. The Irish laborers camped on the Mississippi River between modern Iowa Ave. and Federal St. in an area dubbed "The Patch." The name came from the gardens each family grew. The truth in the advertising of our region is the fact that the Mississippi River Valley is the richest farm soil on planet Earth. The Mississippi River Valley soil is the richest because glaciation. The end of the last Ice Age left the richest topsoil right in the center of the Mississippi

River Valley. Every Midwest resident observes the melting ice each Spring and observes the sediment that remains after the ice melts. The glaciers from the last Ice Age graced the Mississippi River Valley with a magnificent fertile crescent. Regarding the German immigrant experience in the Quad Cities, we must reexamine the persecution German Americans suffered during the World Wars. We believe new immigrants in the Quad Cities can learn from the German and Irish experience and likewise achieve the American dream.

The lessons of German and Irish immigrant hardships in the Quad Cities are relevant when designing our modern urban & regional planning complex systems. The Quad Cities urban regions are seeing a Renaissance of redevelopment from a series of Urban Revitalization laws being codified. Empty buildings are being redeveloped, filled with residents, and raised property values and URTE [Urban Revitalization Tax Exemption]. We are seeing "urban sprawl" models are being replaced with new "urban revitalization and redevelopment" models. The Quad Cities tax base is growing from the manufacture of farm equipment, the cultivation of cash crops and the education industry is experiencing major increases in education clients earning degrees of every kind.[v] The manufacture of farm equipment will continue and grow, although the identity of the Quad Cities is changing because of the influx of new education clients earning degrees.

The education industry is exciting and continually changing. The education industry within our complex system helps build a recession proof community. Recession proof communities are the best environments in which we can design the kinder and gentler society. Research from the Quad Cities Chamber of Commerce reveals 45% of new education clients earning degrees in the Quad Cities are from other regions. Education clients like the Quad Cities education industry. New clients can earn degrees that won't cost an arm and a leg. Even further, the Midwest region is one of the best advertising markets. Marketing and advertising executives realized long ago the Midwest audience is one of the best test audiences. The saying "…if the housewife from Iowa likes the product…" is a remnant from the Eisenhower and Betty Friedan generation that is considered valid and based on real marketing research. In fact, several major marketing, advertising, and entertainment industry firms test market products in the Quad Cities. We will examine the interconnections the Quad Cities is developing with other nations and our identity as an international model of commerce and vacation destination.

Chapter VIII

The Cycle of Poverty in Film

Several modern films portray the cycle of poverty in manners that make poverty "cool." My research and perspectives will debunk the myths and stereotypes of the wealth gap, cycle of poverty and, systemic racism images we see in film. The modern entertainment industry is becoming one of the most influential change agents ever. The advent of film changed the world and continues shaping our perceptions and perspectives. Civilizations built entire empires on entertainment since the earliest tribes. The influence of the modern film and television industry can help urban & regional planners and present planning challenges. Films from the 1990s portrayed several elements of African American "ghettos" [low-income neighborhoods] and exaggerated stereotypes with ticket sales in mind. The entertainment value of such film production liberties is immense. The real social cost is high. Rather than change film production styles that sell movie tickets, we must learn the process of demarcation concerning the realities of the complex systems that cause the wealth gap, cycle of poverty and systemic racism, or end the wealth gap, cycle of poverty and systemic racism.

The film *"Boyz In the Hood"* is a portrayal of the African American "ghetto" culture of youth gangs, guns, violence and drug dealing social problems. Several sources argue that the portrayal of African American low-income neighborhoods is irresponsible and causes real world violence in the suburbs. The film *"Malibus' Most Wanted"* is a clever response from Hollywood regarding the suburban effects of John Singletons' portrayal of the African American low-income neighborhoods. Films portraying African American men as violent thugs and wife beaters are rife with unfair stereotypes. Domestic violence is tragic. Misandry and misogyny are small minded kindergarten playground games. Valerie Jean Solanas' violent assault of Andy Warhol was one moment when the world realized women can be the aggressor. The portrayal of domestic violence in film is almost always portrayed with men as the aggressor. The reality is that domestic violence can be experienced with woman on top as the aggressor or other combinations of partner domestic violence. "Domestic violence is a pressing issue often deemed acceptable by the media, and thus, challenges men and womens' perceptions of how they should "…behave with partners in their relationships."[vi] The rap music lyrics that cause controversy may or may not reflect the community surrounding the rappers.

We can argue that the most objectionable rap lyrics are a result and effect of the cycle of poverty. Several social liberals are apologists regarding the cycle of poverty and defend gritty rap lyrics as being "real." Rap lyrics might reflect the wealth gap, cycle of poverty and systemic racism surrounding the rapper. The truth is that rap as a movement could be an instrument socioeconomic, political, and cultural change. Rappers could change from reflecting the cycle of poverty and projecting the cycle of wealth. We see several rappers projecting images of wealth and privilege. Fancy cars and mansions are found in several modern rap videos. That is an example of changing our perceptions of rappers as exclusively from the cycle of poverty. The power of film imagery can catapult rappers from the cycle of poverty and land them amongst the cycle of wealth. Materialism has become intermingled with rap culture. "…One negative effect of this materialistic expression is that it is not always real. People should express themselves on deeper levels than what car they drive or what diamonds they wear…"[vii] The obsession with materialism in rap music could backfire and become our modern version of *"Putting on the Ritz."* The perception of African Americans as obsessed with materialism has deep roots in our nation. Researching the connections between material obsession and race is an endeavor worth researching.

The 1990s portrayal of African American ghettos was a huge marketing success. Suburban parents with financial resources purchased movies, music, and books at the behest of young children who may never have even seen an African American at school. The movement earned several hundreds of millions. The Hollywood portrayal of the African American ghettos caused huge repercussions until the 21st century. Those effects helped shape white suburban teenagers' perceptions of African American ghettos. The challenge from the urban & regional planning perspective revolves around the issue of class division. Poverty is color blind and the connection between poverty and race remains ever elusive.

Race baiting is a trite strategy that never solves the underlying causes of the wealth gap, cycle of poverty and systemic racism. Race-baiting deflects attention from the origins of the wealth gap, cycle of poverty and systemic racism causing social unrest that ends is quagmires if uncertainty. Deconstructing the stereotypes we see in popular films helps urban & regional planners design new complex systems that end the cycle of poverty regardless of race. The new film *"Parasite"* is receiving interesting reviews regarding the effects of greed and class struggle from the South Korean cultural perspective. Researching cross cultural, multiracial experiences with the cycle of poverty truly reinforces the fact that poverty is color blind.

The glamorization of African American ghettos in film sells movie tickets. The perception of the "coolness" of the cycle of poverty should be considered an ill-conceived marketing ploy. The exploitation of wealthy suburbanites' interest with the "other side of the tracks" was distilled, packaged, and put on the shelves of suburban shopping malls. Further, the explosion of rap music changed the world. Suburban soccer moms became worried. The result was legislation requiring music labels put explicit content warning labels on new music releases. The result helped wealthy suburban consumers at the local mall with purchase decisions. Several sources argue the explicit content warning was a major marketing success because suburban youth culture liked the "dangerous" product image. The ensuing reaction of the rap movement caused new laws. Youth might always identify with being "rebellious" and establishing the proper channels of expression requires the best urban & regional planning. The underlying social problems and themes from rap and hip hop might be elements of the wealth gap, cycle of poverty and/or systemic racism. Freedom of expression is a crucial element of all musical styles. Rappers can and should police themselves and establish what is in the best interests of the genre. Materialistic lyrics and images might damage the perceptions of the rap genre because the origins of the rap movement are from the cycle of poverty.

The entertainment industry exploitation of African American culture is a recurring controversy. The arguments over "blackface," and "blaxploitation" films are debated amongst urban & regional planners. The 1990s films portraying the African American ghetto could be considered the modern "blackface" and "blaxploitation." Several urban & regional planners argue whether the films are realistic or a blatant exploitation of African American stereotypes. One statistic is clear: movie ticket and album sales. Blatant exploitation or realistic portrayal, the products were a commercial success. Urban & regional planners must be "communitycentric" and realize the value and effect of advertising. The Quad Cities is one of the best test regions in the world regarding new products.

Advertising helps shape perceptions and design the best communities. We can learn from the adverse effects of blatant exploitation in the entertainment industry and counter with the best urban & regional planning.

What is the result of the commercially successful exploitation of the wealth gap, cycle of poverty and, systemic racism in film? The exploitation of the African American wealth gap, cycle of poverty and systemic racism saw commercial success. However, urban & regional planners must design new, modern complex systems that end the wealth gap, cycle of poverty and systemic racism. The responsibility is immense. Community members are influenced from several sources that could cloud the process of designing effective complex systems aimed at ending the wealth gap, cycle of poverty and/or systemic racism. Researching relevant examples from popular films can help urban & regional planners design premier cities. Combined with the best, most effective advertising campaigns, urban & regional planners can affect subtle changes within the community.

Racial integration is a red herring when the reality is education empowers new leaders with leadership skills that prevent social unrest. Our nation is becoming a majority multiethnic audience and, we must design new, modern complex systems. We live in a moment of mass shootings and uncertainty. Every individual must understand the origins of the wealth gap, cycle of poverty, and systemic racism, see the signs of social unrest, and design new and better complex systems.

The commercialization of the exploitation of African American ghettos during the 1990s saw the explosion of rap music and film sales at wealthy suburban shopping malls. The real social problem is that members of all communities develop world views that reflect the community in which they reside. We dub such views "communitycentric." The 1990s films and music rap groups like *N.W.A.* earned millions packaging an exploitive image of African American low-income neighborhoods. Wealthy suburban kids purchased the products and filled the movie complexes. The problem from the urban & regional planning perspective is reality. Suburban wealth and community culture is far from the glamorized portrayals of the wealth gap, cycle of poverty and, systemic racism from low-income neighborhoods. The racial friction of community development in our nation is a continuing debate. De facto segregation exists in every nation. Rather than argue the red herring of racism and race-baiting, we must employ the best advertising within our communities. Effective advertising, product placement and development helps builds the communities we want. "Thousands of advertisers "...[design]...separate ethnic marketing strategies..."[viii] These observations might sound trite. However, lack of addressing ethnic marketing would be remiss. Researching ethnic marketing strategies of the emerging electronic cigarette market might be a cool college thesis.

Chapter IX

Intelligently Designing New Complex Systems

Several urban & regional planning firms encounter protests regarding community design. Wealthy community members want certain designs and low-income members want affordable housing designs. The compromise is peculiar because ending the wealth gap, cycle of poverty and/or systemic racism is our plan. We are a capitalist democracy. Affordable housing ideas are complex because they are socialist/communist models. The capitalist market drives the best urban & regional planning development. However, urban & regional planners encounter controversy when designing communities that try and end the wealth gap, cycle of poverty and systemic racism. The low-income housing debate will continue because our capitalist democracy is market driven. Class divisions occur in capitalist systems, socialist systems, and communist systems. Urban & regional planners can and must learn from other world systems of governance. However, we must adhere with our nations' capitalist democracy design. Capitalism is market driven. Diversity, cultural equity, and inclusion arguments based on socialist and communist models of design must be rebuked and funneled through the proper channels. Capitalism is flexible and diversity planning should occur within our nations theme of capitalist democracy. International business laws and large multinational corporations like Apple and McDonalds tax shift across national borders. Several modern researchers believe multinational corporations are effective change agents that minimize the relevance of nationalism. However, the United Nations are developing new international laws that will end multinational corporation tax shifting. Further, nationalistic fervor mixed with socialism and communism is best left in the dust bin of the past and the tragic lessons with such experiments diligently taught in our public schools.

The controversies of urban & regional planning are at once local, regional, national, and international. Each community designs complex systems that solve systemic problems within their specific local community. The best design in South Central Los Angeles could be the opposite of what is best in other regions of our nation. Ending the systemic causes of the cycle of poverty requires an understanding of race and class within the context of complex systems. Racism and race-baiting are red herrings that deflect attention from the complex origins of the wealth gap, cycle of poverty and systemic racism. Poverty is color blind. The connection between poverty and race remains ever elusive. Understanding the fundamentals of capitalism in the modern world helps urban & regional planners address controversies surrounding race and class. Arguing if the entertainment industry is responsible and/or the cause of social problems is small talk at public functions. The explosion of rap music during the 1990s was a marketing success. Successful marketing is some of the best capitalism. Regardless of your rap music collection or lack thereof, the marketing success of rap music was and is a cultural movement.

Why are wealthy suburban high school kids enamored with the exploitation of the film portrayal of the African American wealth gap, cycle of poverty and/or systemic racism? One theory is peer pressure. Peer pressure can be an effective element of successful marketing. We see peer pressure is employed with tremendous success with the advertising of alcohol and cigarettes. That is truly a testimony of the efficacy of advertising. We will explore advertising firms' ethnic marketing plans. Ethnic marketing can shape the self-perceptions of disenfranchised elements of the population. The power of marketing and advertising can help build or damage the individual self-esteem. ***Mattel*** and the ***Barbie*** product are examples of the effect of marketing and advertising peer pressure. Peer pressure regarding body image and photo shopped images of beauty are sometimes targets of ridicule. Regarding ***Barbies'*** beach body measurements, the debate continues while product sales climb. Several researchers contend studies of the effect of the *Barbie* product on self-esteem might exist. However, "…research on this question is surprisingly scarce, and the studies that exist are inconclusive…."[ix] The science of girls' self-esteem becomes even further divided along lines of race, class, and gender. Self-esteem and the search for meaningful empowerment might be a driving force behind some womens' movements.

Several women's studies researchers agree that women's movements encounter divisions along the lines of race, class, and gender. "…White women intentionally…avoid…the continued neglect of, dismissal and, disregard of the issues affecting black women and other women of color."[x] Feminist Frontier pioneers enjoy employing Venn Diagrams that help solve women's studies concerns. Employing visual learning diagrams are an easy method of addressing what divides women and what unites women. Race, class, and gender might be elements of division, whilst biology unites all women with similar experiences. Venn diagram activities are merely the launching point of women studies groups' conversation on issues that affect progress in all interpersonal and public discourse. We are observing women in first world nations in politics and business enjoying a surge of popularity that is being described as the "Third Wave" of feminism. Centrist political scientists argue the most effective women politicians and business leaders in first world nations espouse traditional gender appearance. Women studies groups argue that traditional gender appearance should be irrelevant. A certain young woman politician from New York might be attractive in the traditional sense. However, that should never sway voters regarding the validity of her political message.

Chapter X

Peer Pressure Problems with Urban & Regional Planning

Peer pressure occurs within the milieu of each social class and across race. Films like ***"Valley Girl," "Somekind of Wonderful,"*** and ***"Pretty In Pink"*** are examples of class peer pressure. Rich boy likes poor girl equals social conflict. Rich girl likes poor boy equals social conflict. One theory of the marketing success of the 1990s films from John Singleton could be the cross-class conflicts of youth peer pressure. Wealthy suburban white kids experience conformity peer pressure within the complex system that continues the cycle of wealth. Earn the best scores at school, enter the best colleges, earn the best degrees, land the best jobs, and earn the most wealth. The reality of people experiencing the wealth gap, cycle of poverty and systemic racism is a stark contrast. African Americans experiencing the wealth gap, cycle of poverty and/or systemic racism argue that rap music and films from John Singleton are exploitation that continues the cycle of poverty. "Rappers...speak about structural issues in American society that lead to the problems we still see today in black communities."[xi] Our nation is a capitalistic business. The marketing success of rap music and the 1990s films is a clever, legal capitalistic ploy. However, the unfair exploitation of stereotypes is irresponsible. The urban & regional planning reality of intelligently designing complex systems that end the wealth gap, cycle of poverty and systemic racism must read and understand my theses.

The systemic causes of the cycle of poverty can be influenced with peer pressure. The African American population experiencing the cycle of poverty are influenced with peer pressure. The peer pressure involves a strange pride in poverty. Being "hood" means being poor is cool, hard, and strong. People leaving the complex system of the wealth gap, cycle of poverty and/or systemic racism experience peer pressure. The peer pressure of leaving the "hood" causes cognitive dissonance within the "hood" milieu and is portrayed in Singletons' films with tremendous success. Several professional sports players who entered the pro leagues were from the cycle of poverty. One problem is that sports are perceived as one of the only options African Americans can employ in the war on poverty. Herein are telltale clues of the wealth gap, cycle of poverty, and systemic racism. Sports are valued across race, class, and gender. The wealth gap, cycle of poverty, and systemic racism in African American low-income neighborhoods causes the stereotype that sports are the best option at obtaining wealth. The stereotype that sports are valued above education in African American neighborhoods might be because the educational opportunities are substandard because of our public school funding models. We see several racial stereotypes within the education industry. Asians are science and math experts, and African Americans excel at sports are stereotypes that could be the result of our public school funding models. Understanding the causes of race and education stereotypes involves the dynamics of our public school funding models. Some theorists argue that our public school funding models subconsciously shape young minds regarding self-worth. Changing our public school funding from the property tax pool is against the "community centric" desires of our nation, specifically the archaic 14th Amendment era laws that developed our modern public school funding models. The areas with the largest property tax base build the best facilities. Some lawmakers argue that public school funding could be modified, and we could lower property tax, raise other taxes, and fund public schools from a modified pool of tax money. However, others argue such ideas are radical and arguments in both houses of Congress would end in quagmires of useless debates.

Chapter XI

Public School Funding Models

Public schools are largely funded with property tax. "…Inequality plaguing the public education system…and budget numbers reveal how unfair funding programs dictate what our children are worth, depending on where they live, the color of their skin, and their families' wealth."[xii] Urban & regional planners must be cognizant of the perceived inequality of public school funding. We are a capitalistic democracy. Public schools are funded with property tax. The most expensive property builds the most expensive public schools with the best facilities. Urban & regional planners must research lessons of the Reconstruction, understand the models of public school funding and design the best public school options in line with the larger complex systems of the community. We might never accomplish racial integration and diversity through force. Racial integration and diversity occur naturally when the best urban & regional planning designs become realized.

The backlash against image exploitation of African American low-income neighborhoods is merely an intelligent response from concerned members of the African American community. De facto segregation occurs because racial integration causes social friction. Diversity planning can be one of the most controversial elements when designing the complex systems of our community. Urban & regional planners can employ consulting firms that show due diligence is present when considering diversity, cultural equity, and inclusion. Racial diversity requires proper planning. Successful racial integration of our communities can be challenging, yet our nations' multiethnic majority audience is emerging. "Achieving…diversity…cultural equity and, inclusion is an evolutionary process that will require...intelligently redesigning complex systems. The plan should be considered a living document requiring regular reviews...that change with modern values. The urban & regional plan will be designed on many levels...of leadership, component groups, and member volunteers. This includes an assessment of partnership organizations that help...historically marginalized groups advance diversity and inclusion goals." [xiii]

The exploitation of ethnic stereotypes in popular films changes our culture in ways that produce adverse social effects. We must counter the adverse effects of the exploitation of stereotypes within the entertainment industry and develop clever community planning. The fierce debate regarding gun violence and mass shootings involves blatant blame shifting. The best urban & regional planners realize "...guns don't kill people. Desensitization from...violent video games and..." radical left-wing extremists are the culprit. [xiv] We must understand that combining gun violence with the exploitation of ethnic imagery in film can damage the perceptions of multiethnic groups struggling with identity. Several universities employ films from John Singleton when teaching the social ramifications of the exploitation of African American imagery. We must be cognizant of the subconscious ways in which advertising and media affects the self-esteem of our emerging multiethnic majority audience in our nation.

We might see racial diversity planning within our communities is challenging because the exploitation of racial and ethnic stereotypes in film. Several modern researchers believe the culture of high school "hazing" might be the cause of mass shootings. The aftermath of the Columbine High School shootings saw lawmakers passing wave after wave of antihazing legislation. Changing cultures across racial lines might realize the value of antihazing laws when curbing mass shootings and other violence. The commercial marketing success of such exploitation is merely a reflection of capitalists earning revenue from clever marketing. Hollywood blockbusters are entertainment rather than urban & regional planning designs. Rather than blame the entertainment industry when stereotypical exploitation occurs in film, merely find other examples in film from which we can develop new designs.

Several regions of our nation are in the process of redesigning public school funding models. Understand our public school funding design requires researching Reconstruction. The Civil War divided our nation, and the Reconstruction caused several new Constitutional Amendments. The 14th Amendment provides the provision that whatever isn't mentioned in the Constitution becomes the states right. Public education is a state right. Each state of the nation can design public school funding models. The Civil War ended; however, racial integration struggles continue. School districts are gerrymandered in line with community centric desires. Here we find our complex system designs in earnest. The gerrymandering that occurs with politics reflects the urban & regional planning of our communities. Urban & regional planners find public school funding issues can become political. We must always remember our nation is a capitalistic democracy and our public school funding designs reflect our system of governance.

Most communities in our nation fund public schools with property taxes. Expensive property earns the highest property tax and the public school facilities are superior. "While legally recognized racial segregation…ended…de facto [segregation] remains… Public schools…became…racially diverse in recent decades…as a product of [the]…expansion of the Hispanic school age population. However, the segregation of white from black students has endured."[xv] Understanding our public school funding models will help urban & regional planners counter the adverse effects of the exploitation of racial and multiethnic imagery in popular film.

Our youth earning high school degrees can experience undue influence from media and entertainment. One theory is early neurological development in high school youth might be product of the social class in which they are learning cognition skills. Several behaviorists argue that the cycle of wealth and the cycle of poverty affect neurological development, especially self-esteem and self-worth. Observing the reactions of suburban high school youth when hearing rap and hip hop is the subject of expensive marketing and advertising research studies.

Largely white, wealthy, and suburban high school kids helped launch the careers of several African American rappers. "Systemic and experimental studies on rap music's effects on listeners…is being gathered. Gangster raps' influence on African Americans…and people who never listen or connect with the music…see their lives altered because of rap music. Hip hop is a social movement…and a cultural expression. Hip hop must develop a…philosophy. Hip hop…can cause social change. Gangster rap is a commercialization of hip hop intent on exploiting an audience appetite that wants gangster themes. The hip hop movement is…confused with gangster rap. Hip hop music can be distinguished from gangster rap and should be viewed as its own music genre."[xvi] Urban & regional planners must understand that the rap music genre is a social movement. Social movements are moments from which we can develop new complex system designs. However, social movements alone aren't the most efficient change agents.

Chapter XII

Urban Revitalization and Redevelopment

Changing our public school funding models might be a fierce political debate. If our public schools are funded with property tax, then can we design urban revitalization and redevelopment that increase property values near underfunded schools? Property owners might be reluctant from raising the value of urban blight property because increased property tax. Our urban areas with the lowest property values can approve URTE "Urban Renewal Tax Exemptions" with language like "...any increase in assessed value... from redevelopment...is exempt from...10 years of property taxes..."[xvii]

These kind of city ordinances are changing the identity of our Quad Cities urban regions on both sides of the Mississippi River. Empty buildings are being redeveloped and filled with residents. The residents change the culture and vibe of our Quad Cities urban center, and the new property tax revenue helps fund our public schools in our low-income URTE zones. Scott County provides a wide range of exemptions.[xviii] Our public school funding models are derived from property tax. Urban Revitalization and Redevelopment plans employing URTEs will change the identity, vibe and culture of our urban regions and provide our cities with future property tax revenue funding the public schools in the urban regions.

The politics of public school funding is full of passion and misunderstanding from a public unfamiliar with how our public schools are funded. Revitalization and redevelopment of our nations' urban centers are being researched in our colleges and universities. The Quad Cities, like our entire nation, experienced urban sprawl after the World Wars. The heroes of the World Wars were

guaranteed a safe retirement from the newly
founded social security system. This security
funded "Urban Sprawl." The wars ended when the
Soviet Union collapsed and became one of our
worlds' new democracies. The Cold War ended
and the carnage of the threat of nuclear World Wars
ended. However, the "urban sprawl" funded with
government wartime pensions was unsustainable.
The result is urban center blight. The new
generations are realizing the real estate abutting the
Mississippi River Valley is pure gold. This is why
the new generations are codifying URTEs' and
similar urban revitalization and renewal designs.
Why should the new young generations be denied
access of the Mississippi River real estate because
of the urban sprawl of the Eisenhower generation?
Thankfully, the new generations codified the
URTEs', and we are observing a rebirth of the
urban centers on both sides of the Quad Cities
Mississippi River.

Chapter XIII

Social Movement effects and Complex System designs

Social movements are an American tradition. The Founding Fathers designed the Constitution with rights of free assembly and speech. Some movements establish effective social change, other movements end in quagmires of unrealized potential, and most others fail the original purpose. Regardless of movement success or failure, urban & regional planners can employ unrealized movement potential. One theory regarding movement failure is lack of effective organization. The logistics of masses of citizens peacefully assembled can cause security problems and overshadow the original cause of the movement. Splinters and factions can occur with large masses that cloud the spirit and message of the movement. The other major theory or perspective is that movements are inefficient vehicles of social change. The reality is the best social change occurs within the legislation process. Movements can be effective and cause legislation changes.

Movements are filled with passion and excitement. Passion and excitement are emotions that cause factions within movements. Factions within movements see an otherwise just cause end with the drivel of confused masses. Some argue that the memory of the masses is short, fickle, and merely living in the moment. We can let that debate continue and design communities that empower the new generation with the skills of an individual lobbyist. Thus, if or when an individual becomes enamored with a movement that ends with disappointment, then the individual can employ the skills of an individual lobbyist. The majority of legislation changes occur through the debate process in the legislative branch. Several sources argue that the lobbying process eclipses the efficacy of movements proper. We can affect change with movements, or we can affect change with other styles. Lobbyist can "…influence decision makers. Interest groups…employ lobbying…in the interest of their members. Lobbying…can affect any branch or level of government."[xix]

Movements become inefficient because lack of proper administration and organization. One main argument against movements is the misuse of the popular views of the movement. Movements often use the mass of the populace in furtherance of hidden agendas. The fact is modern citizens can and must become individual lobbyists. The advent of internet surveys and online groups help citizens support causes and never join movements or political parties proper. The argument of the efficacy of modern movements then becomes a matter of the individual becoming the lobbyist. We must embrace social movements as our constitutional providence. The fervor and emotions of movements can cause unnecessary social unrest and even damage property. Urban & regional planners can design communities in which social unrest occurs infrequently. Movements then become inefficient and unnecessary vehicles of change. Movements are often inefficient long term change agents. The best long-term changes are the result of clever urban & regional planning designs.

Chapter XIV

Employing Unrealized Potential from Inefficient
Conglomeration

Every industry learns the process of efficient
agglomeration. Conglomerations can be made
efficient with proper urban & regional planning.
The growing education industry in the Quad Cities
is learning efficient conglomerations with the
agriculture industry and manufacture of *John Deere*
farm equipment and the cultivation of large cash
crops. *Amazon, Kraft,* and *Purina* are large
employers and provide substantial tax base revenue.
The conglomerations between the education
industry and the original tax base industries are an
exciting moment. The Quad Cities could be
considered an "in between" city. Several urban &

regional planners are compiling research on the "cities in between." Cities between 500,000 and 750,000 are the cities in between and require specific planning approaches.[xx]

The Quad Cities region is one of the best advertising test regions in the world. Advertising executives like urban regions like the Quad Cities because researchers can observe consumer product reaction closely. "We continue [believing] test [advertising] is indispensable…and minimizes…the major risks involved in most new product launches."[xxi] Other elements influence consumer behaviors and purchase trends and the Quad Cities can provide the researchers with the best feedback. Large advertising firms enjoy the Quad Cities region when developing new test products because the investment required is within the budget of even the smallest businesses.

The Quad Cities' status as an "in between" city could help the Quad Cities attract and retain talent. Several urban & regional planners lament when our local talent earns degree at university and then leave and obtain employment in other regions of our nation and world. If we research why advertising executives like the Quad Cities as a test marketing region, then that could help local urban & regional planners attract and retain the best talent. Urban & regional planners, the Quad City Chamber of Commerce and Tourism bureaus are developing long range plans increasing the Quad Cities region appeal. Top national and international talent can obtain employment and housing in the Quad Cities and become a member of a premier region leading the world in all kinds of areas.

Chapter XV

Ill Effects of Modern Social Safety Net Programs

Several sources argue modern social safety net programs enables recipients the means of continuing the wealth gap, cycle of poverty and systemic racism. "…Our current…social safety net programs…makes poor people…financially fragile, and [provides] incentives…that encourage welfare recipients…"[xxii] continue receiving welfare assistance. The design of our nations' federal reserve changed the complex systems of the entire world. Several radical left-wing zealots argue that the federal reserve is the cause of certain elements of the cycle of poverty. The reality is the business of our nation is business. If modern social safety net programs cause the wealth gap, generational poverty, and systemic racism, then research must occur proving such hypotheses. We must remember the early Irish & German immigrants escaped the cycle of poverty and entered the cycle of wealth. What is interesting is the early Irish & German immigrants never used the modern welfare system. What can we learn from the early Irish & German immigration experience when researching the cycle of poverty?

Government is government and while elements of the proper function of government contain business elements, our nation at large is one giant business from which government remains independent. The fact of multinational corporations like Apple, McDonalds and Starbucks employing tax shifting when maximizing business revenue is an argument worth researching. Modern research on the wealth gap, cycle of poverty and systemic racism provides urban & regional planners with valuable ideas regarding the effects of tax shifting on employees in our nation. Behaviorists can provide compelling arguments. "…Research shows that the underclass…is most prevalent in urban regions, and mostly racial minorities. Children in these neighborhoods living in poverty lack the kind of role models…that could teach them proper life skills. The challenge is finding ways of providing the poor with generous support and never disregarding unpleasant behaviors."[xxiii]

Several modern urban & regional planners argue a connection between poverty and race. Race is the red herring that can sidetrack relevant research of the causes of the wealth gap, cycle of poverty and systemic racism. Other urban & regional planning researchers debunk behaviorist theories. Role models are cross cultural and cross class. Every social class contains role models regardless of income. The behaviorist argument that children experiencing the cycle of poverty lack proper role models should be admonished.

Chapter XVI

Planning Future Communities with the Elimination of
Ineffective Social Safety Net Programs

The Irish & German immigrants who built the Quad Cities never used modern social safety net programs. We see research that confirms our modern social safety net programs are ineffective and enables the wealth gap, cycle of poverty and systemic racism. The Irish & German immigrants survived and thrived the cycle of poverty. The Irish & German immigrants developed skills on which our nation is founded. "…Irish and German immigrants…built powerful political machines in major metropolitan regions…like Tammany Hall in

New York City and Hibernian Hall in Davenport. These political machines helped new immigrants…providing them with training, opportunities, and even cash…"[xxiv] The most relevant elements of the lessons we learn from the early Irish and German immigrants is the active participation in our system of governance the Founding Fathers designed. "Several politicians support "entitlement reform" including major changes with the federal food-stamps program, or SNAP."[xxv] We are observing the repeal of Medicaid health care laws because the socialist designs are "overreaching" the original spirit of our Constitutional government and themes of capitalism/free enterprise. However, we must maintain a certain level of social safety net programs that prevent the unraveling of society.

Our nation experiences waves of socialist fervor in moments of unrest or uncertainty. The fact is that socialist models of welfare might be popular with some elements of the population. "Socialism is…a system in which the means of production is socially owned. "…Democratically controlled capitalism/free enterprise…ensures the unemployed and poor…attain certain standards that help prevent the disintegration of…the social fabric of capitalist/free enterprise democracy." Politicians like Upton Sinclair and Bernie Sanders are social democrats who want an expansion of the welfare system and larger government regulation of businesses."[xxvi] We see several young movements that believe socialism can end poverty. *Teen Vogue* is among several youth media avenues who entertain socialist movement ideologies. "Ironically, *Teen Vogue* is owned by *Conde Nast*, a company that earns hundreds of millions of dollars…from the capitalist/free enterprise system. Indoctrination of youth with radical socialist ideologies is irresponsible. Capitalism/free enterprise…can end poverty rather than radical left wing extremist ideologists…."[xxvii] Movements are an American tradition. However, we must always suspect the motives of radical left wing socialist movements. The battle over world systems and designs of governance is real.

The colonization of new planets will occur when China embraces free enterprise and democracy. The worlds billions of people can then be employed with unified purpose. Indeed, our destiny is the colonization of new planets. This sounds like science fiction, however Elon Musk and others from our capitalist/free enterprise system are leading the world in these pursuits. We are on the edge of one of the most monumental moments of humankind ever. Capitalism/free enterprise is the light in the darkness leading the new world. The passion and excitement of socialist movements are embroiled in waves of populist fervor. Learning from populist leaders helps urban & regional planners design the best modern complex systems within our capitalist/free enterprise democracy. The Founding Fathers could see the rise of populist leaders might damage the spirit and intent of our system of governance.

Europe is one of our best regions when we are researching populist leaders. The European Union is one of the most modern hybrid designs of social democracy governance. The Soviet Union ended, and Russia became a modern capitalist democracy. Remnants of communism and socialist world systems remain within the new governance systems of the European Union nations. European

Parliament democracy sees coalition governments that embrace some vestiges of communism and socialism. Researching urban & regional planning designs from Europe helps us identify potential desires of labor and the industries providing employment. Our nation and Europe certainly share centuries of experiences. Learning from our respective systems of governance will be one element of designing urban & regional planning systems that can end trade wars and other disagreements that cause international conflicts. *The International Quint Cities Festival* is the oil of diplomacy every nation can employ when designing a new world…a new world with unified purpose, dream, and vision. Establishing the International Quint Cities Festival nonprofit corporation is a good start.

Chapter XVII

Articles of Incorporation

The Executive Producers' Club obtained *the International Quint Cities Festival* articles of incorporation from the Iowa Secretary of State, obtained the EIN [employer identification number] from the IRS and entered the IRS 1023. We will obtain tax exempt status in June 2021. The articles of incorporation are a living document we will change. The reviews of the articles of incorporation are majority vote of the board of directors. Like all nonprofit tax-exempt corporations, we will change the articles of incorporation when we must accomplish certain tasks. The development of the festival will make changes in the articles of incorporation a regular occurrence. Below are the original articles of incorporation of *the International Quint Cities Festival.*

Incorporation, like the U.S. Constitution are living documents and will be changed, amended, and revised when our nonprofit mission changes with whatever modern desires arise in the future.

NONPROFIT ARTICLES OF INCORPORATION
ARTICLE 1, NAME

1.01 Name

a. The name of this corporation will be *"the International Quint Cities Festival."* The business of our public nonprofit tax exempt corporation will be conducted as *"the International Quint Cities Festival."*

    b. The address of the corporation is Bettendorf, Iowa 52722, and Matthew Cepican is the corporation agent.

    c. Incorporator, Matthew CepicanBettendorf, Iowa 52722

d. *"The International Quint Cities Festival"* will be governed with the board of directors. The initial directors of the publicnonprofit corporation are Board Member President, Karen Blomme, Board Member Secretary, Irene Cepican, and Board Member Treasurer, Matthew Cepican, Board Member Vice President Jenna Morehouse.

e.   Distribution of assets upon dissolution will be other nonprofit tax-exempt corporations in the Quint Cities region whose mission is helping the homeless and other vulnerable populations. The revenue from the annual festival each year will be disbursed among nonprofits helping the homeless and other vulnerable populations in the Quint Cities region.

2.01 Purpose

a.   *"The International Quint Cities Festival"* is a nonprofit tax-exempt corporation and will function for public nonprofit tax exempt charitable purposes within the meaning of section 501 (c)(3) of the Internal Revenue Code, or the corresponding section of any future Federal Tax code. *"The International Quint Cities Festival"* purposes are planning an annual festival event on the same day of the *Bix 7* race every year. All proceeds of the festival tshirts, merchandise, tickets and other revenue will be dispersed to the nonprofit tax-exempt corporations named in section 1.01(e). The board of directors will maintain discretion and might provide internships or volunteer opportunities which will be how individuals can become involved with the festival and/or programs developed in conjunction with the festival.

b. Members of the Board of Directors include Karen Blomme, Jenna Morehouse, Matthew Cepican and Irene Cepican.

c. Provisions

(1) The Board of Directors, employees, interns, and volunteers will manage the business of our public nonprofit tax exempt corporation.

(2) The Board of Directors will vote the initial bylaws of *"the International Quint Cities Festival."*

(3) The Board of Directors will be the main voting body of *"the International Quint Cities Festival,"* including the reasonable compensation of the Board of Directors, employees, interns, and volunteers.

d. (1) This is the provision that eliminates or limits the liability of a director to *the International Quint Cities Festival* or its members for money damages, or action taken, or failure to take any action, as a director, except these liability clauses:

(a) Receiving a financial benefit when the director is not entitled.

(b) Intentional infliction of harm on *the*

International Quint Cities Festival or its members.

(c) A violation of section 504.835

(d) Intentional violation of criminal law.

(2) The provision of this paragraph will never eliminate or limit the liability of a director for an act or omission that occurs prior to the effective date of the provision. The absence of a provision eliminating or limiting the liability of a director from this paragraph will never affect the applicabilityof section 504.901.

(e)　　　　　This provision permits or requires *the International Quint Cities Festival* indemnify a director for liability, as definedin section 504.851, subsection 5, to a personfor any action taken, or any failure to take any action, as a director except liability for any of the following:

      (f) Receipt of an unentitled financial benefit.

      (1) Intentional infliction of harm on *the International Quint Cities Festival* and/or its members

      (2) A violation of section 504.835

      (3) Intentional violation of criminal law.

3.01 Nonprofit Nature

"The International Quint Cities Festival" is organized with public nonprofit charitable purposes

including distributions to organizations that qualify as tax exempt organizations under section 501 (c)(3) of the International Revenue Code, or corresponding section of any future federal tax code. The net earnings of *"the International Quint Cities"* will never benefit, or be distributable to its members, trustees, officers, or other private persons, unless *the International Quint Cities Festival* authorizes reasonable compensation for services rendered from employees, interns, volunteers and to make payments and distributions in furtherance of the purposes established in the purpose clause.

"The International Quint Cities Festival" will never carry on any other activities not permitted by any organization exempt from federal income tax under section 501 (c)(3) of the Internal Revenue Code, corresponding section of any futuretax code, or by an organization, contributions to which are deductible under section 170 (c)(2) of theInternal Revenue Code, or corresponding section ofany future federal tax code.

"The International Quint Cities Festival" will never be operated for the private gain of any person. The property of the corporation is irrevocably dedicated to charitable beneficiaries inte

Quint Cities region. The assets, receipts, or net earnings of the nonprofit tax-exempt corporation will never inure, benefit, or be distributed to any individual. *"The International Quint Cities Festival"* may, however, pay reasonable distributions consistent with these articles.

compensation of employees, interns, volunteers regarding services rendered, and payments and

3.02 Prohibited Distributions

"The International Quint Cities Festival" net earnings, or properties of this nonprofit tax exempt corporation, on dissolution or otherwise, will never inure to the benefit of, or be distributableto, its members, directors, officers or other private person or individual, except that *"the International Quint Cities Festival"* is authorized and empoweredto pay reasonable compensation for services rendered and to make payments and distributions infurtherance of the purposes in Article 1.01(e).

3.03 Prohibited Activities

"The International Quint Cities Festival"
will never carry on any activities not permitted of
the International Quint Cities Festival being exempt
from federal income tax as an organization
described by Section 501 (c)(3) of the Internal
Revenue Code, or the corresponding section of any
future federal tax code, or by a corporation,
contributions to which are deductible under Section
170(c)(2) of the Internal Revenue Code, or the
corresponding section of any future federal code.

4.01 Amendments

Amendments of the Articles
of Incorporation may be adopted by
approval of 2/3^{rds} of the board of
directors.

5.01 Addresses

The physical address of *"the
InternationalQuint Cities Festival"*
is Bettendorf, Iowa 52722.

The mailing address of *"the InternationalQuint Cities Festival"* is P.O. Box 526 Bettendorf, Iowa 52722

6.01 Agent

The agent of the corporation is MatthewCepican Bettendorf, Iowa.

7.01 Incorporator

The incorporator of the corporation isMatthew Cepican Bettendorf.

Certificate of Adoption of
the Articles of
Incorporation

I, the undersigned hereby certify that the above stated Articles of Incorporation of *"the International Quint Cities Festival"* were approved by the board of directors on and constitute a complete copy of Articles of Incorporation of *"the International Quint Cities Festival."*

Matthew Cepican,
Bettendorf,
Irene Cepican,
Bettendorf, Iowa
Jenna Morehouse,
Davenport, IA
Karen Blomme,
Davenport, IA

I, Matthew Cepican, agree I am the agent of *"the International Quint Cities Festival"* appointed herein.

Chapter XVIII

Bylaws

Every nonprofit tax-exempt corporation must develop bylaws. The bylaws are the map the nonprofit tax-exempt corporation employs when developing the festival. Below are the original bylaws of our new nonprofit tax-exempt corporation. The bylaws of our public nonprofit tax-exempt corporation will change with our mission. All nonprofit corporations develop a mission, and the mission can and must change with the desires of the board of directors, volunteers, employees, interns, and other individuals in our organizations. The majority vote of the board of directors will make all bylaw changes effective. The bylaws will be changed and revised when *the International Quint Cities Festival* encounters scenarios that are new and come with the changing spirit of the festival. The talent agencies[xi] we might employ relyon the legal, valid contracts *the International Quint Cities Festival* enters. All legal, valid contracts regarding how our grant funds are employed will bediligently seen on the annual IRS 990 document. However, our legal valid contracts with our talentand our contributions list legally remain confidential from the public.

Chapter XVIII
Bylaws
The International
QuintCities
Festival

An Iowa Nonprofit
Corporation

Bylaws

ARTICLE I, Name

1.01 Name

The name of this public nonprofit corporation
is *"the International Quint Cities Festival."* The
business of the corporation may be conducted as
"the International Quint Cities Festival,"
"International QCF," or *"IQCF."*

ARTICLE II, PURPOSES AND POWERS

2.01 Purpose

"The International Quint Cities Festival" is
a public nonprofit tax-exempt corporation and will
be operated for public nonprofit charitable purposes
within the meaning of Section 501 (c)(3) of the
Internal Revenue Code, or the corresponding
section of any future Federal tax code.

The purpose of *"the International Quint
Cities Festival"* is an annual festival planned on the
same day of the Bix 7 race. All revenue from the
festival including tshirts, merchandise, tickets, etc,

shall be disbursed among other nonprofit corporations upon dissolution. The purpose of *"the International Quint Cities Festival"* is an urban and regional planning instrument and will change the ways our Quint Cities region conducts business and develops our underserved communities.

2.02 Powers

"The International Quint Cities Festival" is empowered alone or in conjunction with others regarding all lawful acts that are necessary or convenient to affect the charitable purposes or which *"the International Quint Cities Festival"* is organized and, assist other organizations and persons that accomplish such purposes. The powers of *"the International Quint Cities Festival"* may include, but not limited to, the acceptance of contributions from the public and private sectors of financial or in-kind contributions. All these contributions are subject of applicable laws and the rules established with the IQCF articles of incorporation herein.

2.03 Nonprofit Status and Exempt Activities Limitation

  (a) Nonprofit Legal Status of *"the International Quint Cities Festival"* is an Iowa nonprofit public benefit tax exempt corporation, recognized as tax exempt under Section 501 (c)(3) of the United States Internal Revenue Code.

(b) Exempt Activities Limitation. Directors, officers, employees, members, interns, volunteers, or representatives of *"the International Quint Cities Festival"* will never take any action or carry on any activity by or on the behalf of *"the International Quint Cities Festival"* that is not permitted of an organization exempt under section 501 (c)(3) of the United States International Revenue Code as it exists or may be amended, or by any organization contributions that are deductible under Section 170(c)(2) of such Code and Regulations as it not exists or may be amended. The net earnings of *"the International Quint Cities Festival"* will never benefit or be distributable to any director, officer, member, or other private person, except that *"the International Quint Cities Festival"* shall be authorized and empowered regarding paying reasonable compensation of employees, interns and, other volunteers for services rendered and make payments and distributions in

furtherance of the purposes established in
the Articles of Incorporation and the Bylaws
of *"the International Quint Cities Festival."*

(c) Distribution Upon Dissolution. Upon
termination or dissolution of *"the International
Quint Cities Festival,"* any assets lawfully
available for distribution shall be distributed to
the nonprofit organizations helping the
homeless and other marginalized populations in
the Quint Cities region. The organizations
receiving the assets of *"the International Quint
Cities Festival"* hereunder shall be selected in
the discretion of a majority of the managing
body of *"the International Quint Cities
Festival,"* and if its members cannot agree, then
the recipient organization will be chosen
employing a verified petition in equity filed in a
court of proper jurisdiction against *"the
International Quint Cities Festival,"* by 1 or
more of its managing body which verified
petition shall contain such statements as
reasonably indicate the applicability of this
section. The court can deem this section
applicable and what qualifying organization or
organizations receive assets, giving preference if
applicable to organizations located in the Quint
Cities region. If the court deem this section

applicable but qualifying organization known to it which has a charitable purpose, which, at least generally, includes a purpose similar of *"the International Quint Cities Festival,"* then the court can order the distribution of its assets lawfully available for distribution to the Treasurer of the State of Iowa and added with the general fund.

ARTICLE III, MEMBERSHIP

3.01 Membership Classes

"The International Quint Cities Festival" shall not allow members any right to vote or title or interest in or to *"the International Quint Cities Festival,"* its properties and franchises.

3.02 Nonvoting Affiliates

The board of trustees might vote and grant classes of nonvoting affiliates with rights, privileges, and obligations established by the board. Affiliates may be individuals, businesses, and other organizations that support the mission of *"the International Quint Cities Festival."* The board, a designated committee of the board, or an elected officer in accordance with board policy, will enjoy authority to admit any individual or organization as an affiliate, recognize representatives of affiliates, and determine the affiliates' rights, privileges, and obligations. The affiliates' information will never be shared or sold to other organizations or groups unless first obtaining the signed permission of the affiliate. The board of trustees can vote, and proposed affiliates might be given endorsement, recognition and media coverage at fundraising activities, clinics, other events or at *"the International Quint Cities Festival"* website. Affiliates are nonvoters and are not members of *"the International Quint Cities Festival."*

3.03 Dues

Any dues for affiliates shall be determined by the board of trustees.

ARTICLE IV, BOARD OF TRUSTEES
4.01 Number of Directors

"The International Quint Cities Festival" will employ a board of trustees consisting of at least 3 and never more than 15 board members. The board may add or subtract the number of directors serving on the board, including for the purpose of staggering the terms of trustees.

4.02 Powers

All public nonprofit tax exempt corporation powers will be exercised by or under the authority of the board and the affairs of *"the International Quint Cities Festival"* will be managed under the direction of the board unless law provides otherwise.

4.03

(a) All trustees shall be elected to serve a one-year term, however, the term may be extended until a successor is elected.

(b) Trustee terms will be staggered such that approximately 2/3rds of the trustees will end their terms in any given year.

(c) Trustees may serve terms in succession.

(d) The term of office shall be considered from January 1st and end December 31st of the second year in office unless the term is extended until a successor is elected.

4.04 Qualifications and Election of Trustees

The board of trustees' eligibility requirements include the following: the individual must be 18 years of age and an affiliate as classified by the board of trustees. Trustees may be elected at any board meeting by the majority vote of the existing board of trustees. The election of trustees shall be in January of each year.

4.05 Vacancies

The board of trustees might fill vacancies at the expiration of a trustees' term of office, resignation, death, removal of a trustee or may appoint new trustees that fill a previously unfilled board position, subject to the maximum number of trustees under these bylaws.

    (a) Unexpected vacancies. Vacancies in the board of trustees from resignation, death, or removal shall be filled by the board of trustees for the balance of the term of the trustee being replaced.

4.06 Removal of Trustees

A trustee may be removed by 2/3rd vote of the board of trustees then in office, if:

(a) The trustee is absent and unexcused from two or more board of trustees voting sessions in a twelve-month period. The board of president can excuse directors from attendance if the reason is deemed adequate by the board president. The president will not be empowered regarding excusing herself/himself from the board voting session and in that case, the board treasurer or vice president shall excuse the president.

(b) If prior of a board voting session at which a vote on removal will be made the trustee in question is given electronic or written notification of the boards intention to discuss her/his case and is given the opportunity to be heard at a voting session of the board.

4.07 Board of Trustees Voting Sessions

(a) Regular voting sessions. The board of trustees will enjoy a minimum of between 1 and 4 regular voting sessions each calendar year at times and places decided by the board. Board voting sessions will occur with a minimum of 7 days' notice by first class mail, electronic mail, fax, or 7 days' notice delivered personally or by telephone. If sent by mail, fax, or electronic mail, the notice shall be deemed to be delivered upon its deposit in the mail, email, or fax system. Notice of board voting sessions will specify the place, day, and house of the board voting session. The specific purpose of the board meeting is never required.

(b) Special voting session. Special voting sessions of the board may be called by any member of the board of trustees. A special voting session must be preceded by at least 7 days' notice to each trustee of when, where and what time, but specifying the purpose is never required.

(c) Waiver of Notice. Any trustee may waive notice of any meeting, in accordance with Iowa law.

4.08 Manner of Acting

(a) A majority of the trustees in office immediately before a board voting session will constitute a quorum and transact business at that board voting session. Business will never be considered by the board at any voting session at which a majority of trustees is not present.

(b) Majority Vote. Except as otherwise required by law or by the articles of incorporation, the act of the majority of the trustees present at a board voting session shall serve as agreement of the subject of the vote.

(c) Hung Board Decisions. If the directors of the board lack consensus based on a tied vote, then the president or the treasurer maintain discretion and are empowered with a swing vote.

(d) Participation. Except as required otherwise by law, the Articles of Incorporation, or these bylaws, trustees may participate in a regular or special voting session using any means of communication by which all directors participating may simultaneously receive communication from other board members during the meeting, including in person, electronic communication, internet video meeting or by telephonic conference call.

4.09 Compensation for Board Member Services

The board of trustees may adopt policies providing for reasonable reimbursement of trustees' expenses incurred in conjunction with board responsibilities, [i.e. travel expenses when attending board voting sessions, etc.]

4.10 Compensation for Professional Services by Trustees

Trustees can be renumerated for professional services provided *"the International Quint Cities Festival."* Such renumeration will be reasonable and fair with respects of *"the International Quint Cities Festival"* and must be reviewed and approved in accordance with the board Conflict of Interest policy and Iowa law.

ARTICLE V, COMMITTEES

5.01 Committees

The board of trustees can, with resolution adopted by a majority of the trustees in office, designate one or more committees, each consisting of two or more trustees that will serve at the pleasure of the board. Committees, provided in resolutions of the board, will enjoy all the authority of the board, except

(a) Expend corporate funds to support a nominee for trustee; or

(b) Amend or repeal bylaws or adopt new bylaws.

(c) Committees may never take final action that requires board members approval of a majority of all members.

(d) Committees may never fill vacancies on the board of directors in any committee which has the authority of the board.

(e) Amend or repeal any resolution of the board of trustees the terms of which cannot be repealed or amended.

(f) Appoint any other committees of the board of trustees or the members of these committees.

(g) Approve any transaction:

i.   *"The International Quint Cities Festival"* is a party and one or more directors have a material financial interest; or

ii.   Between *"the International Quint Cities Festival"* and one or more of its trustees or between the corporation and persons in which one or more of the trustees receive material financial interest.

Action of Committees

Committees' actions will be governed employing the provisions of Article IV of these bylaws regarding voting session of the trustees, with such changes in the bylaws necessary to substitute the committee and its members for the board of trustees and its members, except that the time for regular action of the committees may be determined with resolution of the board of trustees or resolution of committees. Special action of the committees may be called with resolution of the board of trustees. Notice of special action of committees shall also be given to all alternate members, who enjoy rights of attending all actions of the committee. Minutes are kept of each action of committees and put with *"the International Quint Cities Festival"* records. The board of trustees might employ rules regarding the governing of the committee consistent with the provision of these bylaws.

Informal Action by the Board of Trustees

Any action required or permitted to be taken by the board of trustees at a voting session are considered valid in the absence of the presence of board members if consent in writing, setting forth the action, shall be agreed by consensus of the majority of the board of trustees. Email from an email address on record constitutes a valid writing. This provision allows the board of trustees employing email when approving action if the board of trustees' majority agree with such decision.

ARTICLE VI, OFFICERS

6.01 Officers of the Corporation

The officers of *"the International Quint Cities Festival"* are the board president, vice president, secretary, and treasurer, all of whom shall be chosen by, and serve at the pleasure of, the board of trustees. Each board officer is empowered with authority and will perform the duties detailed in these bylaws, with resolution of the board or by direction of an office authorized by the board to prescribe the duties and authority of the officers. The board can appoint additional vice presidents and such other officers as necessary regarding the proper business conduct of *"the International Quint Cities Festival.,"* each of whom enjoys authority and performs such duties as the board of directors might approve. One person may maintain two or more board offices, but board officers will never act in more than one capacity where action of two or more officers is required.

6.02 Terms of Office

Each officer shall serve a 1-year term of office and may not serve more than 7 consecutive terms of office. Unless unanimously elected by the board at the end of his/her 7th year or to fill a

vacancy in an officer position, each board officers'
term of office shall begin upon the adjournment of
the board voting session at which elected and shall
end upon the adjournment of a board meeting when
a successor is elected.

6.03 Removal and Resignation

The board of trustees might remove officers
at any moment. Officers may resign at any time by
giving *the International Quint Cities Festival*
written notice and will never forfeit rights, if any, of
the International Quint Cities Festival and
contract(s) of which the officer is a party.
Resignations are effective upon receipt notice or at
any time specified in the notice, unless otherwise
specified in the notice. Resignations are effective
and never require acceptance of the other board
members.

6.04 Board President

The board president shall be the chief
volunteer officer of *the International Quint Cities
Festival.* The board president will lead the board

of trustees in performing duties and responsibilities, including, if present, presiding at all voting sessions of the board of trustees, and will perform all other duties of the office or properly required by the board of trustees.

6.05 Vice President

If the board president is absent, then the ranking president designated by the board of trustees can commandeer the responsibilities of the board president. The vice president will enjoy all the powers of the board president. The vice president will enjoy all the powers of and subject to all the restrictions upon the board president if the president is absent. The vice president enjoys other powers and performs duties that are prescribed them from the board of trustees or the board president. The vice president shall accede to the office of the board president upon the completion of the board presidents' term of office.

6.06 Secretary

The secretary keeps the book of minutes of all board voting sessions and actions of directors and committees of directors. The minutes of each voting session will contain time, place, and other information necessary regarding what action occurred in accordance with the law and these bylaws. The secretary gives other board members copies of the minutes from the voting session as required by the bylaws. The secretary shall enjoy powers and perform such duties as may be prescribed by the board of directors or the board president. The secretary might appoint, with approval of the board, a trustee to assist in performance of all or part of the responsibilities of the secretary.

6.07 Treasurer

The treasurer will be the lead trustee regarding oversight of the financial condition and business of *"the International Quint Cities Festival."* The treasurer will oversee and keep the board informed of the financial condition of *"the International Quint Cities Festival"* and of audit or financial review results. In conjunction with other trustees or officers, the treasurer shall oversee budget preparation and shall ensure that appropriate financial reports, including an account of major transactions and the financial condition of *"the International Quint Cities Festival,"* are made available to the board of trustees on a routine basis or as required by the board of trustees. The treasurer will perform all duties properly required by the board of trustees or the board president. The treasurer may appoint, with the approval of the board a qualified fiscal agent or member of the staff to assist in performance of all or part of the duties of the treasurer.

6.08 Non-Trustee Officers

The board of trustees might appoint additional officer positions of *"the International Quint Cities Festival"* and might appoint and assign the duties of other non-trustee officers of *"the International Quint Cities Festival."*

ARTICLE VII, CONTRACTS, CHECK, LOANS

INDEMNIFICATION AND RELATED
MATTERS

7.01 Contracts and other Writings

The indemnification of *"the International Quint Cities Festival"* is provided herein except resolution of *"the International Quint Cities Festival"* board of trustees or board policy that all contracts, deeds, leases, mortgages, grants, and other agreements of *"the International Quint Cities Festival"* will be executed on its behalf by the treasurer or other persons with whom *"the International Quint Cities Festival"* delegated authority to execute such documents in accordance with policies approved by the board.

7.02 Checks, Drafts

Checks, drafts, and other orders for payment of money, notes, or other evidence of indebtedness issued in the name of *"the International Quint Cities Festival,"* shall be signed by such officer or officers, agents, or agents, of *"the International*

Quint Cities Festival" and in such manner as determined from resolution of the board of trustees.

7.03 Deposits

All funds of *"the International Quint Cities Festival"* not otherwise employed shall be deposited to the credit of *"the International Quint Cities Festival"* in banks, trust companies, or financial institutions as the board or designated committees of the board may select.

7.04 Loans

Loans will never be contracted on behalf of *"the International Quint Cities Festival"* or evidence of indebtedness issued in the name *"the International Quint Cities Festival"* unless authorized by resolution of the board. Such authority might be general or confined to specific instances.

7.05 Indemnification

(a) *"The International Quint Cities Festival"* will indemnify a trustee or former trustee, who was successful, on the merits or otherwise, in the defense of any proceeding of which she or he was a party because she or he was a trustee of *"the International Quint Cities Festival"* against reasonable expenses incurred by her or him in connection with the proceeding.

(b) *"The International Quint Cities Festival"* will indemnify a trustee or former trustee who is/was a party of a proceeding because she or he is or was a trustee of *"the International Quint Cities Festival,"* against the liability incurred in the proceeding, if the determination to indemnify her or him has been made in the manner prescribed by the law and payment has been authorized as codified in the law.

(c) Expenses incurred in defending a civil or criminal action, suit or proceeding may be paid by *"the International Quint Cities Festival"* in advance of the final disposition of such action, suit or proceeding, as authorized by the board of trustees in specific cases, upon receipt of a written affirmation from the trustee, officer, employee or agent of his or her good faith belief that he or she is entitled to indemnification as authorized in the article, and an undertaking by or on the behalf of the trustee, officer, employee or agent to repay such amount, unless it is determined that he or she is entitled to be indemnified by *"the International Quint Cities Festival"* in these bylaws.

(d) An officer of *"the International Quint Cities Festival"* who is not a trustee is entitled to mandatory indemnification under this article same as a trustee. *"The International Quint Cities Festival"* may also indemnify and advance expenses to an employee or agent of *"the International Quint Cities Festival"* who is not a trustee, consistent with Iowa law and public policy, provided that such indemnification, and the scope of such indemnification, is established with the general or specific action of the board or by contact.

ARTICLE VIII, MISCELLANEOUS

8.01 Books and Records

"The International Quint Cities Festival" will maintain books and records of account of the

proceedings of all voting sessions of its board of trustees, a record of all actions of the board of trustees, and a record of all actions of committees of the board. In addition, *the International Quint Cities Festival"* shall maintain a copy of *"the International Quint Cities Festival"* Articles of Incorporation and Bylaws as newly amended.

8.02 Fiscal Year

The fiscal year of *"the International Quint Cities Festival"* is from January 1st until December 31st of each year.

8.03 Conflict of Interest

The board will adopt and periodically review a Conflict-of-Interest policy to protect *"the International Quint Cities Festivals'"* interest when contemplating any transaction or arrangement which may benefit any director, officer, employee, affiliate, or member of a committee with board delegated powers.

8.04 Nondiscrimination Policy

The officers, trustees, committee members, employees, and persons served by *"the International Quint Cities Festival"* will be selected entirely on a nondiscriminatory basis with respect to age, sex, race, religion, national origin, and sexual orientation. It is the policy of *"the International Quint Cities Festival"* never discriminates based on age, physical disability, veterans' status, political service or affiliation, color, religion, or national origin. The diverse, cultural equity and inclusive language is always changing, and *"the International Quint Cities Festival"* will always change and revise our language in line with the proper, modern language of diversity, cultural equity, and inclusion.

8.05 Bylaw Amendment

These bylaws might be amended, altered, repealed, or restated by a majority vote of the board of trustees then in office at a voting session of the board, provided, however,

(a) Amendments of these bylaws would never be voted and changed that would cause *"the International Quint Cities*

Festival" to cease to qualify as an exempt organization under section 501(c)(3) of the International Revenue Code, or the corresponding section of any future Federal Tax Code; and,

(b) That an amendment never affects the voting rights of trustees. An amendment that affects the voting rights of trustees further requires ratification by 2/3rd vote of the board of trustees at a board voting session.

(c) That all amendments be consistent with the Articles of Incorporation.

ARTICLE IX

COUNTERTERRORISM AND DUE DILIGENCE POLICY

The tax-exempt contributions to other organizations, domestic or foreign of *"the International Quint Cities Festival"* will stipulate how the funds will be used and shall require the recipient to provide *"the International Quint Cities Festival"* with detailed records and financial proof of how the funds were employed.

"The International Quint Cities Festival" willfully adopts the U.S. charities best practice, protocols, guidelines, and suggestions that reduce, develop, reevaluate, and strengthen a risk-based approach that guard against the threat of diversion of charitable funds or exploitation of charitable activity by terrorist organizations and their support networks.

"The International Quint Cities Festival" will comply with the federal guidelines, suggestion, laws, and limitation established with preexisting U.S. legal requirements related to combating terrorist financing, which include, but are not limited by, various sanctions programs administered by the Office of Foreign Assets Control (OFAC) regarding its foreign activities.

ARTICLE X, DOCUMENT RETENTION POLICY

10.01 Purpose

The purpose of this document retention policy is establishing standards of document integrity, retention, and destruction and promoting the diligent retention of *"the International Quint Cities Festival"* documents.

10.02 Policy

Section 1

Records will be destroyed if they are not
needed for the operation of the business or required
by law. Unnecessary records should be eliminated
from the files. The cost of maintaining records is an
expense which can grow unreasonably if proper
management lapses. A mass of records also makes
it more difficult when obtaining pertinent records.

"The International Quint Cities Festival"
might establish retention or destruction policies or
schedules for specific categories of records in order
to ensure legal compliance, and accomplish other
objectives, such as preserving intellectual property
and cost management. Categories of documents
that warrant special consideration are indemnified
below. Retention periods are established, however
retention of the documents identified below and of
documents not included in the identified categories
should be determined from the general guidelines
affecting document retention, as well as the
exception for litigation relevant documents and any
other pertinent factors.

Section 2

"The International Quint Cities Festival" expects all officers, trustees, and employees will comply fully with any published record retention or destruction policies and schedules, provided that all officers, trustees and employees should observe the following general exception to any stated destruction schedule: If you believe, or *"the International Quint Cities Festival"* informs you that corporate records are relevant to litigation, or potential litigation (i.e. a dispute that could result in litigation), then you must preserve those records until it is determined that the records are irrelevant and could be destroyed. That exception supersedes any previously or subsequently established destruction schedule of documents that are never pertinent in the operation of the business.

Section 3

(a) Corporate records include the corporations' Articles of Incorporation, Bylaws, and IRS form 1023 and Application for Exemption. Corporate records should be retained permanently. IRS regulations require that the form 1023 be available for public inspection upon request.

(b) Tax records include, but may not be limited to, documents concerning payroll, expenses, proof of contributions made by donors, accounting procedures, and other documents concerning *"the International Quint Cities Festivals'"* revenues. Tax records should be retained for at least seven years from the moment of filing the applicable return.

(c) State and federal statutes require *"the International Quint Cities Festival"* maintain certain recruitment, employment, and personnel information. *"The International Quint Cities Festival"* should maintain personnel files that reflect performance reviews and any complaints brought against *"the International Quint Cities Festival"* or individual employees under applicable state and federal statutes. *"The International Quint Cities Festival"* should maintain in the employees personnel file all final memoranda and correspondence reflecting performance reviews and actions taken by or against personnel. Employment applications should be retained for three years. Retirement and pension records should be kept permanently. Other employment and personnel records should be retained for seven years.

(d) Board voting session minutes should be retained in perpetuity in *"the International Quint Cities Festival"* minute book. A clean copy of all other board and board committee materials should be maintained a minimum of three years.

(e) *"The International Quint Cities Festival"* should retain permanent copies of all press releases and publicly filed documents under the theory that *"the International Quint Cities Festival"* should maintain copies that can test the accuracy of any document a member of the public can theoretically produce against *"the International Quint Cities Festival."*

(f) Legal counsel should be conducted when determining the retention period of particular documents, but legal documents should generally be maintained for a period of ten years.

(g) *"The International Quint Cities Festival"* will maintain copies of marketing and sales documents of the same period it maintains other corporate files, generally three years. An exception of the three-year policy may be sales invoices, contracts, leases, licenses, and other legal documentation. These documents should be maintained for at least three years beyond the life of the agreement.

(h) Development documents are subject of intellectual property protection in their final form (e.g. patents and copyrights). The documents detailing the development process are of value regarding *"the International Quint Cities Festival"* and protected as a trade secret where *"the International Quint Cities Festival"*

    i.   Derives economic value from the secrecy of the information; and

    ii.   Developed processes that keep the information confidential

(i) Legal copies of all contracts entered by *"the International Quint Cities Festival"* should be retained. *"The International Quint Cities Festival"* should retain copies of the final contracts for at least three years beyond the life of the agreement, and longer in the case of contracts filed regarding the business of the public nonprofit corporation.

(j) Unless correspondence falls under other categories listed elsewhere in this policy, correspondence should generally be saved three years.

(k) Accounts payable ledgers and schedules should be kept for seven years. Bank reconciliations, bank statements, deposit slips and checks (unless for crucial payments and purchases) should be maintained three years. Any lists of products, materials, and supplies and any invoices should be kept seven years.

(l) Expired insurance policies, insurance records, accident reports, claims, etc. should be maintained permanently.

(m) External audit reports should be kept permanently. Internal audit reports will be kept three years.

Section 4

Email that must be saved should be either:

1. Printed in hard copy and kept in the appropriate file; or

2. Downloaded to a computer file and kept electronically or on disk as a separate

file. The retention period depends upon the subject matter of the email, as covered elsewhere in this policy.

ARTICLE IX

TRANSPARENCY AND ACCOUNTABILITY

DISCLOSURE OF FINANCIAL INFORMATION WITH THE GENERAL PUBLIC

11.01 Purpose

"The International Quint Cities Festival" will make full and accurate information about its mission, activities, finances, and governance publicly available, *"the International Quint Cities Festival"* practices and encourages transparency and accountability of the members of the general public. This policy will:

1. Indicate which documents and materials produced by *"the International Quint Cities Festival"* are presumptively open to staff and/or the public.
2. Indicate which documents and materials produced by *"the International Quint Cities Festival"* are presumptively closed to staff and/or the public.

3. Specify the procedures whereby the open/closed status of documents and materials can be altered.

The details of this policy are as follows:

1. *"The International Quint Cities Festival"* will provide its Internal Revenue forms 990, 990T, 1023 and 5227, bylaws, conflict of interest policy, and financial statements regarding inspection free of charge at the request of the general public.

2. *"The International Quint Cities Festival"* shall make widely available the aforementioned documents on its international website www.internationalqcf.org whence the documents can be viewed from members of the general public

   (a) The documents will be posted in a format that allows and individual using the internet to access, download, view and print them in a manner that exactly reproduces the image of the original document filed with the IRS (except information exempt from public discourse requirements, such as contributor lists).

(b) The website will clearly inform readers the document is available and provide instructions for downloading it.

(c) *"The International Quint Cities Festival"* will never charge a fee for downloading the information. Documents will never be posted in a way that would require special computer hardware or software (other than software readily available to the public free of charge).

(d) *"The International Quint Cities Festival"* will advise any individual requesting the information where this information can be found, including the web address. This information must be provided immediately for in person requests and within 7 days for mailed requests.

11.04 IRS Annual Information Returns (f990)

"The International Quint Cities Festival" will submit the f990 to its board of trustees prior to the filing of the f990. While neither the approval of the f990 or a review of the f990 is required under Federal law, the corporations' f990 will be submitted to each member of the board of trustees

via hard copy or email at least 10 days before the f990 is filed with the IRS.

11.05 Board

1. All board deliberations shall be open to the public except where the board passes a motion to make any specific portion confidential.

2. All board minutes shall be open to the public once accepted by the board, except where the board passes a motion to make any specific portion confidential.

3. All papers and materials considered by the board will be open to the public following the voting sessions at which they are considered, except where the board passes a motion to make any specific paper or material confidential.

11.06 Staff Records

1. All staff records will be available for consultation by the staff member concerned or by their legal representative.

2. Staff records will never be made available to any person outside *"the International Quint Cities Festival"* except the authorized government agencies.

3. Withing *"the International Quint Cities Festival,"* staff records will be made available only to those persons with managerial or personnel responsibilities for that staff member, except that staff records shall be made available to the board when requested.

11.07 Donor Records

1. All donor records will be available for consultation by the members and donors concerned or by their legal representatives.

2. Donor records will never be made available to any other person outside *"the International Quint Cities Festival"* except the authorized governmental agencies.

3. Within *"the International Quint Cities Festival,"* donor records will be made available only to those persons with managerial or personnel responsibilities for dealing with those donors, except that donor records shall be made available to the board when requested.

ARTICLE XII

CODES OF ETHICS AND WHISTLEBLOWER POLICY

12.01 Purpose

"The International Quint Cities Festival" requires and encourages trustees, officers and employees observe and practice high standards of business and personal ethics in the conduct of their duties and responsibilities. The employees and representatives of *"the International Quint Cities Festival"* must practice honesty and integrity in fulfilling their responsibilities and comply with all applicable laws and regulations. The intent of *"the International Quint Cities Festival"* must adhere with all the applicable laws and regulations regarding *"the International Quint Cities Festival."* The purpose of this policy is supporting *"the International Quint Cities Festivals'"* goal of legal compliance. The support of all corporate staff is necessary regarding achieving compliance with various laws and regulations.

12.02 Reporting Violations

If any trustee, officer, staff or employee reasonably believes that some policy, practice, or activity of *"the International Quint Cities Festival"* is in violation of law, a written complaint must be filed by that person with the vice president or the board of trustees' president.

12.03 Acting in Good Faith

Any individual or organization filing a complaint concerning a suspected violation must be acting in good faith and establish reasonable grounds for believing the information disclosed indicates a violation. Allegations that prove not to be substantiated and which prove to have been made maliciously or knowingly to be false will be subject to civil and criminal review.

12.04 Retaliation

The complaining party is protected from retaliation only if she/he brings the alleged unlawful activity, policy, or practice to the attention of *"the International Quint Cities Festival"* and provides *"the International Quint Cities Festival"* with a reasonable opportunity to investigate and correct the alleged unlawful activity. The protection described below is only available to individuals that comply with this requirement.

"The International Quint Cities Festival" will never engage in retaliation against any trustee, officer, staff or employee who in good faith, has made a protest or raised a complaint against some practice of *"the International Quint Cities Festival"* or some other individual or entity with whom *"the*

International Quint Cities Festival" has a business relationship, on the basis of a reasonable belief that the practice is in violation of the law, or a clear mandate of public policy.

"The International Quint Cities Festival" will never engage in retaliation against any trustee, officer, staff or employee who disclose or threaten to disclose to a supervisor or a public body, any activity, policy, or practice of *"the International Quint Cities Festival"* that the individual reasonably believes is in violation of a law, or a rule, or regulation mandated pursuant to law or is in violation of a clear mandate of public policy concerning the health, safety, welfare, or protection of the environment.

12.05 Confidentiality

Violations or suspected violations may be submitted on a confidential basis by the complaint or may be submitted anonymously. Reports of violations or suspected violations shall be kept confidential to the extent possible, consistent with the need to conduct an adequate investigation of suspected violations of the business of *"the International Quint Cities Festival."*

12.06 Handling of Reported Violations

The board president or vice president will advise the sender and acknowledge receipt of the reported violation or suspected violation within five business days. All reports shall be promptly investigated by the board and its appointed committee and appropriate corrective action shall be taken if warranted by the investigation.

This policy shall be made available to all trustees, officers, staff or employees and they shall have the opportunity to ask questions about the policy.

ARTICLE XIII, AMENDMENTS OF ARTICLES OF INCORPORATION

13.01 Amendment

Amendments of the Articles of Incorporation will be adopted by approval of 2/3rd of *"the International Quint Cities Festival"* board of trustees.

CERTIFICATE OF ADOPTION OF BYLAWS

I hereby certify that the above stated bylaws of *"the International Quint Cities Festival"* were approved by *"the International Quint Cities Festival"* board of trustees on 09/10/2020 and are a complete copy of the bylaws of *"the International Quint Cities Festival."*

Irene Cepican, Secretary

Chapter XIX

IQCF Conflict of Interest Policy and Agreement

"The International Quint Cities Festival" developed a conflict-of-interest policy and agreement. Below is the original conflict of interest policy. The conflict-of-interest policy helps protect the board of trustees, employees, interns, and volunteers from potential legal action regarding revenue from the public nonprofit corporation. Conflicts of interest could occur with mismanagement of nonprofit corporation funds. Diligent and proper management of our nonprofit tax-exempt corporation is governed with the laws of

all nonprofit tax-exempt corporations. The good news is all nonprofit tax-exempt corporations must make publicly available the nonprofit corporation financial documents. The legal public observation of nonprofit tax-exempt corporations helps the public trust the business of the nonprofit tax-exempt corporation.

CONFLICT OF INTEREST POLICY AND AGREEMENT

ARTICLE I, PURPOSES

"The International Quint Cities Festival" trustees, officers, and are aware that both real and apparent conflicts of interest sometimes occur in the course of conduction the affairs of *"the International Quint Cities Festival"* and that the appearance of conflict can be troublesome even when there is absence of conflict. Conflicts occur because the many persons associated with *"the International Quint Cities Festival"* should be expected, and generally possess several interests and affiliations and various positions of responsibility within our community. These

instances could see an individual owing identical duty of loyalty. The purpose of the conflict-of-interest policy is protecting the corporations' tax-exempt interest when contemplating voting a transaction or arrangement that might benefit the private interest of an officer or trustee of *"the International Quint Cities Festival"* or might result in a possible excess benefit transaction. The policy is intended to supplement but never replace any applicable state and federal laws governing conflict of interest applicable to nonprofit and charitable organizations.

Conflicts potentially or might place the interests of others ahead of *"the International Quint Cities Festival"* obligations to its charitable purposes and the public interest. Conflicts could reflect adversely upon the person involved and upon the institutions with which they are affiliated, regardless of the facts of motivations of the parties. The long-range best interests of *"the International Quint Cities Festival"* never require the termination of all association with persons who might develop real or apparent conflicts that are harmless to all individuals or entities involved.

Each member of the board of trustees and the staff of *"the International Quint Cities Festival"* enjoys a duty of loyalty regarding *"the International Quint Cities Festival."* The duty of loyalty generally entails a trustee or staff member prefer the interests of *"the International Quint Cities Festival"* rather than that of the trustees or staffs' interest or the interests of others. In addition, trustees and staff of the corporation shall avoid acts of self-dealing which may adversely affect the tax-exempt status of *"the International Quint Cities Festival"* or cause any sanction or penalty by a governmental authority.

ARTICLE II, Definitions

Interested Person

Any trustee, principal officer, or member of a committee with governing board delegated powers, who has direct or indirect financial interest, as defined below, is an interested person.

Financial Interest

A person has a financial interest if the person has, directly or indirectly, through business, investment, or family:

(a) An ownership or investment interest in any entity with which *"the International Quint Cities Festival"* is a party of a legal, valid contract, transaction, or arrangement,

(b) A compensation arrangement with *"the International Quint Cities Festival"* or with any entity or individual with which *"the International Quint Cities Festival"* is a party of a legal valid contract, transaction, or arrangement, or

(c) A potential ownership or investment interest in, or compensation arrangement with, any entity or individual with which *"the International Quint Cities Festival"* is negotiating a transaction or arrangement.

Compensation includes direct and indirect renumeration as well as gifts of favors that are substantial. A financial interest is not

necessarily a conflict of interest. Under
Article III, Section 2, a person who has a
financial interest might develop a conflict of
interest only if the appropriate governing
board or committee decides that a conflict of
interest exists.

ARTICLE III, PROCEDURES

3.1 Duty to Disclose

Interested persons must disclose the
existence of the financial interest and be given the
opportunity to disclose all material facts to the
trustees and members of committees with governing
board delegated powers considering the proposed
transaction or arrangement in connection with any
actual or possible conflict of interest.

3.2 Determining if a Conflict of Interest Exists

Interested persons will leave the governing
board or committee session after disclosure of the
financial interest and all material facts, and after
any discussion with the interested person, while the
determination of a conflict of interest is discussed

and a vote is obtained. The remaining board or committee members shall decide if a conflict of interest exists.

3.3 Procedures for Addressing the Conflict of Interest

(a) An interested person may make a presentation at the governing board or committee session, but after the presentation, she/he shall leave the session during the discussion of, and the vote on, the transaction or arrangement involving the alleged conflict of interest.

(b) The chairperson of the governing board or committee shall, if appropriate, appoint a disinterested person or committee to investigate alternatives to the proposed transaction or arrangement.

(c) The governing board or committee shall determine, after exercising due diligence, if *"the International Quint Cities Festival"* can obtain with reasonable efforts a more advantageous transaction or arrangement from a person or entity that would not give rise to a conflict of interest.

(d) If a more advantageous transaction or arrangement is not reasonably possible under circumstances not producing a conflict of interest, the governing board or committee shall determine by a majority vote of the disinterested trustees if the transaction or arrangement is in *"the International Quint Cities Festivals'"* best interest, for its own benefit, and if it is fair and reasonable. In conformity with the above determination, it shall make its decision if *"the International Quint Cities Festival"* should enter the transaction or arrangement.

3.4 Violations of the Conflicts of Interest Policy

(a) If the governing board or committee establishes reasonable cause to believe a member has failed to disclose actual or possible conflicts of interest, the board of trustees will inform the member an opportunity to explain the alleged failure to disclose.

(b) If, after hearing the members' response and after making further investigation as warranted by the circumstances, the governing board or committee determines the member has failed to disclose an actual or possible conflict of interest, the board of trustees will take appropriate disciplinary and corrective action.

ARTICLE IV, RECORDS OF PROCEEDINGS

4.1 Minutes

The minutes of the governing board and all committees with board delegated powers shall contain:

(a) The names of the person who disclosed or otherwise found to have a financial interest in connection with an actual or possible conflict of interest, the nature of the financial interest, any action taken to determine if a conflict of interest was present, and the governing board of committees' decision if a conflict of interest in fact existed.

(b) The names of persons who were present for discussions and votes relating to the transaction or arrangement, the content of the discussion, including any alternatives to the proposed transaction or arrangement, and a record of any votes taken in connection with the proceedings.

ARTICLE V, COMPENSATION

5.1 A voting member of the governing board who receives compensation, directly or indirectly, from *"the International Quint Cities Festival"* for services is precluded from voting on matters pertaining to that members' compensation.

5.2 A voting member of any committee whose jurisdiction includes compensation matters and who receives compensation, directly or indirectly, from *"the International Quint Cities Festival"* for services will never vote on matters involving that members' compensation.

5.3 Voting members of the governing board or any committee whose responsibility includes compensation matters and who receives compensation, directly or indirectly, from *"the International Quint Cities Festival,"* either individually or collectively, may provide information to any committee regarding compensation.

ARTICLE VI, ANNUAL STATEMENTS

Each trustee, principal officer, and member of a committee with governing board delegated powers shall annually sign a statement which affirms such person:

(a) Has received a copy of the conflicts of interest policy,

(b) Has read and understands the policy,

(c) Has agreed to comply with the policy, and

(d) Understands that *"the International Quint Cities Festival"* is a public nonprofit charitable corporation and in order to maintain its federal tax exemption it must engage primarily in activities which accomplish one or more of its tax-exempt purposes.

ARTICLE VII, PERIODIC REVIEWS

Regular reviews will be conducted that ensure *"the International Quint Cities Festival"* operates consistently with public nonprofit tax-exempt corporation charitable purposes and never engage in activities that could revoke tax-exempt status. The regular reviews will include the following subjects:

(a) If compensation arrangements and benefits are reasonable, based on competent survey information and the result of arms' length bargaining.

(b) If partnerships, joint ventures, and arrangements with management corporations conform to *"the International Quint Cities Festivals'"* written policies, are properly recorded, reflect reasonable investment or payments for goods and services, further charitable purposes and do not result in unreasonable benefit, forbidden private benefit or in an excess benefit transaction.

ARTICLE VIII, USE OF OUTSIDE EXPERTS

"The International Quint Cities Festival" may, but never require, employing outside advisers when conducting the periodic reviews as provided for in Article VII. If outside experts are employed, their employment will never relieve the governing board of responsibilities ensuring periodic reviews are conducted.

CERTIFICATE OF ADOPTION OF CONFLICT-OF-INTEREST POLICY

I certify that the above stated Conflict of Interest Policy and Agreement for *"the International Quint Cities Festival"* were adopted by the board of trustees on 09/10/2020 and constitute a complete copy of the Conflicts-of-Interest Policy of *"the International Quint Cities Festival."*

Irene Cepican, Secretary

Chapter XX

The International Quint Cities Festival Mission

Every nonprofit tax-exempt corporation must develop a mission. Below is the original mission of *"the International Quint Cities Festival."* The board of trustees might change the mission phrase with each regular review of the public nonprofit festival corporation. The mission of nonprofit tax-exempt corporations is like a slogan, tagline, or other marketing instrument that furthers the purposes of the organization. *"The*

International Quint Cities Festival will revise and modify the mission when modern desires arise, and while the mission might evolve, the purpose of the original mission remains. Nonprofit missions can and must change because new, modern complex systems are always changing.

The International Quint Cities Festival

Mission

We are developing a diverse, inclusive Quint Cities region.

Organizational Structure

Board of Trustees

Karen Blomme, Jenna Morehouse, Matthew Cepican, Irene Cepican

Products, Programs, Services

Our first nonprofit project will be
developing an annual festival on the same day of
the Bix 7 race. The festival will build the Quint
Cities region as a destination. Other nonprofit
corporations in the Quint Cities region helping the
homeless will receive the proceeds of the festival,
including tshirt, merchandise and ticket sales. The
festival will contain several elements including live
music, films, food, and other media arts. *The
International Quint Cities Festival"* nonprofit tax-
exempt corporation will employ residents of the
Quint Cities homeless shelters on the day of the
festival every year.

Marketing Plan

Our audience will be all ages. The festival
is multivenue, multimedia, and multithemed.
Obtaining grants, donations and individual tax-
deductible contributions and other funding will help
us attract the best music talent and license the best
films. The festival will build the Quint Cities
region and develop the Quint Cities as an
international destination. The inland port of the
Quint Cities Mississippi River valley will obtain

national port status. Every port in our nation drives commerce. The unrealized potential of the Quint Cities port region is why we are all here after all. Every Quint Cities resident observes the daily barge traffic through all the lock and dam system. Like the Bix 7 race, we will market the festival on the international stage. *"The International Quint Cities Festival"* believes most of the Quint Cities residents want our vulnerable, marginalized populations reentering the mainstream population. We see a lot of volunteers at the Quint Cities homeless shelters who are eager in helping the underserved populations.

However, we believe our wealthiest population might be uncomfortable volunteering with our marginalized populations because the cross-class culture shock of extreme poverty. The annual festival will be a fun, inclusive and diverse event with an emphasis on cultural equity that all classes can attend. Other nonprofit corporations in the Quint Cities region will receive thsirt sales, and merchandise and ticket revenue. Thus, every festival attendee can be confident the event will be an annual way everybody can help our vulnerable, marginalized, and underserved populations.

Operational Plan

We will obtain grants and other funding and attract the best music talent and license the best films. We will obtain employees who contact the music talent and film talent and sign legal, valid contracts with the talent. Like the RME, the IQCF Foundation Group will be involved with music, however, our mission is the rehabilitation of homeless adults and veterans in the Quint Cities. We will employ residents of the QC homeless shelters every year at the festival and give our most vulnerable populations an inclusive and diverse employment chance.

Evaluation Plan

The evaluation will be the development of the annual festival brand including website, app, merchandise, etc.

Management and Organizational Team

"The International Quint Cities Festival" board of trustees will hire employees necessary in obtaining the music and film talents. Film licensing and musician performance agreement contracts will be elements of the festival planning. Employees and volunteers will help with the festival organization on the day of the IQCF. We will employ residents of the QC homeless shelters every year at the festival. The inclusive, diverse plan with an emphasis on cultural equity, will build the community and give our most vulnerable populations employment chances.

Capitalization

We are a debt free startup. We will obtain funding from grants, other business, and individual tax-exempt charitable contributions.

Financial Plan

Obtain funding from grants, businesses, and individual tax-exempt charitable contributions. We will build *"the International Quint Cities Festival"* in this fashion. We will draw the best music, food, filmmaker talent and develop multiple venues in the Quint Cities region. Funding from grants, businesses and individual tax-exempt contributions will help our nonprofit tax-exempt corporation obtain building space with a community stage musicians can employ all year long between festivals. The festival marketing plan will build an inclusive, diverse QC region. Every major corporation in the world can and must develop diverse, inclusive world views with an emphasis on cultural equity.

Chapter XXI

Articles of Incorporation Acknowledgement

Every new nonprofit tax-exempt corporation must enter the original articles of incorporation with the Secretary of State of the state in which the new nonprofit corporation is being developed. Below is the acknowledgement from the Iowa Secretary of State. Our sincere desire is individuals develop nonprofit corporations when changing complex systems.

IOWA SECRETARY OF STATE

No: FT0075114

504RDN-643048

The International Quint Cities Festival

ACKNOWLEDGEMENT OF DOCUMENT
FILED

The Secretary of State acknowledges the receipt of the following document:

Articles of Incorporation

The document was filed on Sep 29th, 2020, at 7:10 AM, to be effective as of Sept 29th, 2020 10:07 AM.

The amount of $20.00 was received in full payment of the filing fee: 09/29/2020

Paul D. Pate
Secretary of State

Chapter XXII

EIN [Employer Identification Number]

Every new nonprofit corporation must obtain an EIN [employer identification number]. Below is a copy the original EIN from the IRS.

DEPARTMENT OF THE TREASURY
INTERNATION REVENUE SERVICE
CINCINNATI, OH 45999-0023

Date of this notice 09/29/2020
Employer Identification Number [EIN] 85-3229427

Form SS-4

Number of this notice CP 575A

INTERNATIONAL QUINT CITIES FESTIVAL
% Matthew James Cepican
BETTENDORF, IA

You may call us at: 1-800-829-4933

If you write, attached the stub at the end of this
notice.

WE ASSIGNED YOU AN EMPLOYER
IDENTIFICATION NUMBER

Thank you for applying for an Employer
Identification Number [EIN]. We assigned you EIN
85-3229427. This EIN will identify you, your
business accounts, tax returns, and documents, even
if you have no employees. Please keep this notice
in your permanent business records.

When filing tax documents, payments, and
related correspondence, you must use your EIN and
complete name and address exactly as shown above.
Any variation may cause a delay in processing,

result in incorrect information in your account, or even cause you to be assigned more than one EIN.

If the information is not correct as shown above, please make the correction using the attached tear off stub and return it to us.

Based on the information received from you or your representative, you must file the following forms(s) by the date(s) shown.

Form 941 10/31/21
Form 940 1/31/2022

Questions regarding the form(s) and the due date(s) shown, you could call us at the phone number or write to us at the address shown at the top of this notice. If you need help in determining your annual accounting period (tax year), see Publication 538, Accounting Periods and Methods. We assigned you a tax classification based on information obtained from you or your representative. It is not a legal determination of your tax classification and, is not binding on the IRS. If you want a legal determination of your tax classification, you may request a private letter ruling from the IRS under the guidelines in Revenue Procedure 2004-1, 2004-1 I.R.B. 1 (or superseding Revenue Procedure for the year at issue). Note:

Certain tax classification elections can be requested by filing Form 8832, Entity Classification Election. See Form 8832 and its instructions for additional information.

If you are required to deposit for employment taxes (Forms 941, 943, 940, 944, 945, CT-1, or 1042), excise taxes (Form 720), or income taxes (Form 1120), you will receive a Welcome Package shortly, which includes instructions for making your deposits electronically through the Electronic Federal Tax Payment System (EFTPS). A Personal Identification Number (PIN) for EFTPS will also be sent to you under separate cover. Please activate the PIN once you receive it, even if you have requested the services of a tax professional or representative. For more information about EFTPS, refer to Publication 966, Electronic Choices to Pay All Your Federal Taxes. If you need arrangements with your Financial Institution to complete a wire transfer.

(IRS USE ONLY) 575A 09-29-2020 INTE B 9999999999 SS-4

The IRS is committed to helping all taxpayers comply with their tax filing obligations. If you need help completing your returns or meeting your tax obligations, Authorized e-file Providers, such as Reporting Agents (payroll service providers) are available to assist you. Visit the IRS Web site at www.irs.gov for a list of companies that offer IRS e-file for business products and services. The list provides addresses, telephone numbers, and links to their web sites.

To obtain tax forms and publications, including those referenced in this notice, visit our website at www.irs.gov. If you do not have access to the internet, call 1-800-829-3676 (TTY/TDD 1-800-829-4059) or visit your local IRS office.

Keep a copy of this notice in your permanent records. This notice is issued only one time and the IRS will not be able to generate a duplicate copy for you. You may give a copy of this document to anyone asking for proof of your EIN. Use this EIN and your name exactly as they appear at the top of this notice on all your federal tax forms. Refer to this EIN on your tax-related correspondence and documents.

If you have questions about your EIN, you can call us at the phone number or write to us at the address shown at the top of this notice. If you write, please include the stub at the bottom of this notice and send it along with your letter. If you do not need to write us, do not complete and return the stub. Your name control associated with this EIN is INTE. You will need to provide this information, along with your EIN, if you file your returns electronically. Thank you for your cooperation.

Keep this part for your records. CP 575 A (Rev. 7-2007)

....Return this part with any correspondence so we may identify your account. Please CP 575 A correct any errors in your name or address. 9999999999 Your Telephone Number Best Time to Call DATE OF THIS NOTICE: 09-29-2020 ( ) – EMPLOYER IDENTIFICATION NUMBER: 85-3229427

FORM: SS-4 INTERNAL REVENUE SERVICE CINCINNATI OH 45999-0023

INTERNATIONAL QUINT CITIES FESTIVAL
% Matthew James Cepican
BETTENDORF, IA

Chapter XXIII

The IRS 1023 Document

Every new nonprofit must enter the IRS 1023 document when obtaining tax-exempt status.[xxviii] The IRS 1023 document is accessible, and you must research the document.[xxix] Ending the war on poverty and developing new complex systems is hard. Nonprofit corporations are a clever way we can end the wealth gap, cycle of poverty and systemic racism.[xxx] Every nation on Earth can end the wealth gap, cycle of poverty and systemic racism. The largest music concerts ever help raise awareness of good causes.[xxxi] However, my observation is the starving musician/artist stereotype is a fact. The coolest bands we all love came through town, packed the venue, and then slept in their cars after the concert. That might sound cliché, but that is the truth. What then is the answer? The answer is developing a new nonprofit festival. The tax-exempt status lets us obtain arts foundation grants and then our talent can earn a living.

     "The International Quint Cities Festival" design is special. Rather than a large crowd at one site like the Mississippi Valley Fair Grounds, we are developing the entire QC region. Our festival will be everywhere at once. Every music venue will be full of every kind of music and art. The festival traffic will be in every town of the QC. Developing the festival on the same day of the Bix 7 race is the best plan. The Bix 7 race is really the QC reunion every year. The Executive Producers Club is merely building on our Bix 7 race tradition. The traffic of the festival will help every small business around each venue.

Chapter XXIV

The Grants Mosaic 2022

Tax exempt 501(c)(3) nonprofit corporations are eligible of obtaining grant funding. Grant funding helps nonprofit corporations accomplish their mission. The IQCF mission is developing a diverse, inclusive QC region with an emphasis on cultural equity. "…If you are…ineligible…regarding specific funding opportunities, you would waste a lot of time and money completing…grant…applications…when you are ineligible…

Regarding eligibility,…you must identify what organization you represent…the IQCF is a nonprofit organization.

Nonprofits with a 501(c)(3) status with the Internal Revenue Service (IRS), other than institutions of higher education

Nonprofits that do not have a 501(c)(3) status with the IRS, other than institutions of higher education…"[xxxii]

The IQCF is a 501(c)(3) nonprofit tax-exempt corporation and eligible regarding grant funding.

There are lots of local grant opportunities here in the Quad Cities region. Here is a small list of local foundation groups and grantmaking organizations here in the Quint Cities who help fund the mosaic of nonprofit corporations building our region.

- QC Community Foundation

- East Moline Foundation

- Hubbell Waterman Foundation

- Quad City Arts

- Rotary Club of Rock Island

- Teens for Tommorrow

- Paint Iowa Beautiful

- Roy J. Carver Charitable Trust

- United Way
- Bechtel Trusts & Foundation [Scott County]
- American Legion of Iowa
- Regional Development Authority
- Illinois Arts Council
- BiState Literacy Council
- Scott County Regional Authority
- Moline Rotary
- Arconic
- Moline Foundation
- HavLife
- Iowa Womens' Foundation
- Rotary Club of Rock Island
- Iowa Arts Council
- Iowa Historic Resource Development
- Illinois Humanities Council
- Roy J. Carver Charitable Trust
- Humanities Iowa
- Doris and Victor Day Foundation
- Rauch Family Foundation
- Rock Island Community Foundation

- Illinois Humanities Council

- Bettendorf Rotary

- Brissman Foundation

- CRST International

- RI Gaming Council

- Iowa Tourism

- Koch Foundation

- Travel Iowa

This is just a small list of the local and regional grant making foundations and groups. Diligence is researching how each local foundation disburses grant funds each cycle.

Travel Iowa[xxxiii] is a grant making organization and helps nonprofit groups build Iowa tourism. The IQCF likes building tourism with our annual festival event. Travel Iowa was "…thrilled to receive a great response…regarding the FY2022 grant…program. Travel Iowa…received 77 eligible applications seeking $557,500 in grant funding. A team of industry peers dedicated many hours…and carefully reviewed and assessed each application to determine successful applicants. Below is the list of the 40 grant recipients for fiscal year 2022.

- Adams Community Economic Development Corporation

  o 2022Marketing

- Ames Convention & Visitors Bureau

  o "This is Ames" tourism video

- Black Hawk County Conservation

  o Black Hawk County Parks Guide

- Butler-Grundy Development Alliance

  o Rolling Prairie Bike Trail Marketing

- Cedar Falls Tourism & Visitors Bureau

  o Cedar Falls Early Spring Digital Ads in MN and WI

- Charles City Tourism

  o CharlesCityTradeshowBoostfor2022

- Chrono Pop LLC dba AnimeCon.org

  o Anime-zing! Japanese Anime Culture Convention

- City of Dubuque, Office of Arts & Cultural Affairs

- o Communications Campaign for Dubuque's Arts & Culture Sector

- Clayton County Development Group

  o Advertising NE Iowa on Television

- Clear Lake Area Chamber of Commerce

  o Targeted Digital + Video Marketing Campaign

- Corning Opera House Cultural Center

  o Video Ads

- Council Bluffs CVB

  o 2022 Council Bluffs Shoulder-Season Marketing Initiative

- Danish Windmill

  o Statewide Local Cable Advertising Campaign

- Decorah Area Chamber of Commerce

  o A Sense of Community

- Dysart Development Corporation

  o Discover Dysart

- Estherville Area Chamber of Commerce

  o Emmet County Water Trail Kayak Rentals

- Friends of the Festival Foundation dba Orange

City Tulip Festival

  o 2022TulipFestivalMarketing

- Grace on Main, LLC

  o Social Media Outreach

- Greater Muscatine Chamber of Commerce and
Industry

  o Downtown Muscatine Banner Project •
  Honey Creek Creamery, Inc.

  o TV and Radio Advertising - Honey Creek
  Creamery, Inc.

- Hoover Presidential Foundation

  o Increasing Tourism with Hoover's

Hometown Days
- Jackson County Area Tourism Association

  o Grant Wood Scenic Byway: Engaging
  Visitors with NEW Maps

• Jackson County Iowa Fair Association

    o JCFA Online Marketing Campaign

• Julien Dubuque International Film Festival o JDIFF Marketing & Promotion

• Lake View Community Club

    o City of Lake View Television Advertising

• Launch PAD Children's Museum

    o Discover Siouxland's play destination,

    the hidden gem of Northwest Iowa!"[xxxiv]

"Philanthropy starts early at the Quad Cities Community Foundation. The Community Foundations Teens for Tomorrow [T4T] gives Quad Cities High Schools the opportunity to experience the grantmaking process firsthand, awarding real dollars to local nonprofits....

The following nonprofits received this years Teens for Tomorrow grants:

- Hope at the Brick House, to enhance education of highly at-risk elementary-age children $750

- Humility Homes and Services, for stability funds for housing relief $1500
- Martin Luther King Jr. Center, for its after-school program $2500
- Mary Lee House of Refuge, for its self-sufficiency program $3000
- Tapestry Farms, to invest in the lives of refugees and their children $2500
- The Literacy Connection, for TLC summer school $500
- Love Girls Magazine, for mentoring and literacy $1000
- Project Renewal, for its 2022 summer youth program $2000
- Testimonies of Hope, for holistic resources for youth survivors of domestic violence $750
- Youth Service Bureau of Rock Island County, for its summer coping camp $1000"[xxxv]

The Quad City Community Foundation awarded $475,000 in scholarships in the 2022 grant cycle.[xxxvi] Supporting our local scholars helps build our community.

"…The Quad City Community Foundation in conjunction with the Hubbell-Waterman Foundation grants $1.2 million to 43 nonprofits. The following nonprofits received grants from the Hubbell-Waterman Foundation:

- Ballet Quad Cities: Using ballet building social literacy, emotional learning, and self-expression in Quad Cities Youth $25,000
- Figge Art Museum: Education Programs $50,000
- Mississippi Valley Blues Society: Blues in the Schools, Augmenting History and Music Education with Blues Performances and workshops $5000
- Quad City Arts: Arts Dollars 2022 $80,000
- QCSO: Operational Support $20,000
- Quad Cities Community Broadcasting Group, Inc.: Access to Opportunity$15000
- River Music Experience: InTune: Building Futures with Music Mentoring $20,000
- SBC Outreach Music & Arts Academy: Office Operations $5000
- The Deanery School of Music: Operational Support in our Crucial Foundational Stages $50,000
- Fresh Films: Yearly Learning, Skill-Building & Career Program for At-Risk Quad City Teens $9000
- Girl Scouts of Eastern Iowa and Western Illinois: The Girl Scout Leadership Experience for Girls in Scott and Rock Island Counties $30,000

- Hope at the Brick House, Inc.: Enhancing Learning for At-Risk Children $10,000
- Junior Achievement of the Heartland: Inspiring Tomorrows Today: JA Biztown and JA Finance Park Learning Experiences $18,000
- Junior Theatre: Breaking Down Barriers: Shows are Free for All to See $8000
- Putnam Museum and Science Center: the Putnam Reimagined $140,000
- Spring Forward Learning Center: Developing Literacy Rates for At-Risk East Moline-Moline Elementary Students $30,000
- WQPT Quad Cities PBS-WIU Foundation: Education and Outreach Services $50,000
- YMCA of the Iowa Mississippi River Valley: Camping Counts: Chance for Success $25,000
- Argrows House: Critical Equipment $23,940
- Boys & Girls Clubs of the Mississippi River Valley: Operational Support $20,000
- Café on Vine: Daily Readiness Program $6000
- Child Abuse Council: Child Abuse Prevention and Community Education $20,000
- Family Resources, Inc.: Survivor Services and Victims of Crime Support $40,000
- Grow Quad Cities Fund Iowa: Quad Cities Career Connections Program: Apprenticeship Signing Day $10,000
- Hand in Hand: Pre-K expansion $41,000

- Heart of Hope Community Outreach Ministries: Wings to Fly Higher $20,000
- LivWell Cares: Free Personalized Placement, information & referral services for low-income seniors in the QCA $6000
- NAMI Greater Mississippi Valley: Development Operations Support $30,000
- Narratives QC: Empowering At-Risk Young Adults to Reach Their Full Potential $10,000
- One Eighty: Workforce Training for At-Risk Davenport Residents $15,500
- Project Renewal of Davenport: Summer Youth Program $8500
- Q2030: Quad Cities Regional Vision $40,000
- Quad Cities Open Network: QCON-SEAP $25,000
- Quad Cities Open Network: Zero Suicide $50,000
- Riverbend Food Bank: Expanding to End Hunger Capital Campaign $20,000
- Riverbend Food Bank: Backpack Program $60,000
- Safer Foundation: Youth Empowerment Program [YEP] support $25,000
- School Health Link: Program Support for Youth Healthcare Services $10,000
- Tapestry Farms: Investing in the Lives of Refugees in the Quad Cities $10,000

- The Martin Luther King Center: Operational Support $30,000
- Unity House: Safety and Security of Unity House Residents in the West 8th Street House $8000
- Vera French Foundation: Sustainability & Expansion to Reach More At-Risk Youth $75,000
- Youth Service Bureau of Rock Island: Peer Justice Program $15,000"[xxxvii]

These are the local and regional groups who received funding from the QC Community Foundation and Hubbell-Waterman Foundation in the summer 2022 cycle.

The East Moline Foundation granted $230,000 to nonprofit groups in the Summer 2022 cycle. Here is the list of grant recipients from the "…East Moline Foundation:

- Abbey Foundation: Capital Building $5000
- Association of Fundraising Professionals: Program Support $2500
- American Red Cross of America: Home Fire Prevention and Relief $2500
- Argrow's House of Healing and Hope: Client Support Services $7500
- Bethany for Children and Families: Teen Programming $7500

- Boys and Girls Club of the Mississippi Valley: Program Support $5000
- Crime Stoppers of the Quad Cities: Gun Buy Back Program $2500
- Dress for Success: Career Connections Program $2500
- Every Child: Prevention Services $5000
- Family Museum of Arts and Sciences: Thomas and Friends Summer Programming $2500
- Figge Art Museum: Big Picture Outreach $2500
- First Tee Quad Cities: Program Support $2500
- Friends of Hauberg Civic Center: Capital Support $4000
- Genesius Guild: Midsummers Night's Dream Production Costs $2500
- German American Heritage Center: Programming Support $1000
- Gilda's Club Quad Cities: Technology Upgrades $3000
- Gigi's Playhouse: Technology Upgrades $2500
- Habitat for Humanity: Low-Income Homeowners Support $7500
- Heart of Hope Ministries: Capital Project Support $3000

- Humilities Homes and Services: Rapid Rehousing Program $5000
- Jamieson Community Center: Mercer County Senior Services $5000
- Living Proof Exhibit: Program Support $2500
- Mercado on Fifth: New Community Center $10,000
- Midwest Writing Center: Young Emerging Writers Internships $2500
- Moline 150: Sesquicentennial Celebration Support $15,000
- Moline Township: Summer Concert Series $2500
- Nest Café: Food Costs $8500
- Playcrafters Barn Theatre: Roof replacement $8000
- Prairie State Legal Services: Program Support $4000
- Pregnancy Resources: Safety First Car Seat Program $2500
- Quad Cities Open Network: QCON Program Support $2500
- Quad Cities Botanical Center: Ability Garden $2500
- Riverbend Food Bank: Expanding to End Hunger $25,000
- SAL Family and Community Services: Milan Facility Playground $10,000

- STEAM on Wheels: MLK Jr. Center Program $10,000
- Trust First Film Alliance: Resurrecting Forest Grove Production $2500
- Two Rivers YMCA: Summer Camp $10,000
- Wilson Middle School: Family Reading Program $1500
- Youth Services: Bureau of Rock Island County Program Support $4000
- Youth Hope Christian Friendliness: HVAC repairs $7500"xxxviii

The Doris & Victor Day Foundation in Rock Island, Illinois is one of the premier grant-making foundations in the Quad Cities region. Doris & Victor Day cared about the well-being of the people of the Quad Cities, especially residents of Rock Island. It has been the responsibility of the trustees to make the vision of a "better place" a reality in the Quad Cities. Here is a list of the Day Foundation grants from Summer 2022:

- 100 Black Men Quad Cities, Inc. HBCU Civil Rights College Tours $10,000
- American Red Cross Disaster Relief Services $3500
- Association of Fundraising Professionals Quad Cities: Empowering Quad Cities Fundraisers and Strengthening the Nonprofit Community $1000

- Augustana College: Speech, Language, and Hearing Scholarships $2500
- Augustana College Prison Education Program at East Moline Correctional Center $3000
- Azubuike African American Council for the Arts: Voice & Vision Theatre for the Black Diaspora $3000
- Ballet Quad Cities: Expansion of Ballet Quad Cities' educational outreach programming to 5th grade
- Bethany for Children & Families: Equipping teens with tools for a healthy body and mind in a post pandemic world.
- Big Brothers Big Sisters of the Mississippi Valley: Parent engagement initiative
- Black Hawk College Foundation: Adult Education GED Testing Fees
- Café on Vine: Providing service to our most vulnerable community members in the QC area
- CASI: Center for Active Seniors: Senior Wellness Program Development
- Child Abuse Council: Child Abuse Prevention and Educational Services
- Children's Therapy Center of the Quad Cities, NFP: Therapy for Children Living in Rock Island whose families are unable to afford the cost.
- Christian Care: General Operations-Marthas House Community Meal Site
- Clock, Inc.: Clock Inc.

- Community Caring Conference: Community Building-Next Level
- Figge Art Museum: Big Picture arts engagement in the schools and in the community
- First Tee of the Quad Cities: Program Equipment at the Highland Springs Golf Course
- Friends of Hauberg Civic Center Foundation: Repurposing the Hauberg Carriage House for Nature play based on day care and STEAM Educational Classroom
- Genesius Theatre Foundation: Directors for the 2023 Season
- German American Heritage: Speaking Truth to Power: the White Rose Resistance and Holocaust Lesson for Today
- Hand-in-Hand: Hand in Hand Sensory Walk
- Heart and Hope Ministries: Giving the Gift of Life
- Humility Homes and Services, Inc.: Humility Homes and Services, Inc.: Rapid Rehousing Program
- Iowa Abortion Access Fund: Iowa Abortion Access Fund
- IWLC: 2022 Quad Cities Leadership Conference and Women in Leadership Awards
- Kinnas House of Love Inc.: Kinnas Corner
- LeadHer: Strike a Match Mentor Recruitment
- LivWell CARES: Free Placement, Information & Referral Services for Low Income Seniors in Rock Island County

- Lutheran Socials Services of Illinois: Quad Cities Childrens Services basic needs fund
- Marriage and Family Counseling Service: Insuring Access to Therapy for All Quad Cities Families
- NAACP Branch #3268: Rock Island County National Association for the Advancement of Colored People (NAACP) #3268
- Nahant Marsh Education Center: Operational Support
- Narratives: Empowering at-risk Young Adults to Reach Their Full Potential through Life Coaching
- NEST Café (Nourish Everyone Sustainably Together): General Operating Funds
- Prairie State Legal Services: 2022 General Operating Expense for Prairie State Legal Services
- Putnam Museum and Science Center: Education access fund
- QC Community Broadcasting Group: Access to opportunity
- Quad Cities Open Network, the Hub: QCON-Supplemental Emergency Assistance Program [SEAP]
- Quad City Arts, Inc.: 2022-2023 Visiting Artists Series
- Quad City Botanical Center: Core Operating Support

- Quad City Symphony Orchestra: QCSO Music Education Access Programs
- Rock Island County Children's Advocacy: Problematic Sexual Behavior Program
- Rock Island Kiwanis Foundation: Rock-Island Milan First Day Fund
- Rock Island-Milan Education Foundation: Rock Island-Milan First Day Fund
- Rock Island-Milan Education Foundation: Promoting Rock Island-Milan Education Foundation 2022-2023
- Rocky Resource Room: Rock Resource Room at Rock Island High School
- Rotary Club of Rock Island: Hope in the Streets Mural of Mentoring
- Safer Foundation: Safter Foundation— Employment Services Program
- SBC Music & Arts Academy: SBC Outreach Music and Arts Academy
- Spring Forward Learning Center: Increasing out-of-school Time Programs as a Response Strategy
- STEAM on Wheels: Using STEAM Instruction to Build Better Writers
- Tapestry Farms: Urban Farming to Invest in the Lives of Refugees
- The Literacy Connection: The Literacy Connection Operating Expenses 2022-2023 School Year

- The Martin Luther King Center: Martin Luther King Center Operations
- The Salvation Army of the Quad Cities: Operating for Community
- Transitions Mental Health Services: A Brand-New Day-Tele psych Services in our Community
- Trinity College of Nursing & Health Sciences: Scholarships for Underrepresented Students
- Western Illinois University Foundation: Degree Attainment Assistance
- World Relief: Refugee Health and Wellness Program
- WVIK, Quad Cities NPR: WVIK, Quad Cities NPR Programming Support
- Youth Services Bureau of Rock Island County: Youth Service Bureau Family Therapy Program

This is just a small list of grant recipients from the QC Community, Regional Development Authority (RDA), Hubbell Waterman Foundation, and the East Moline Foundation. Reviewing the list, you can see the "Grant Mosaic" of our Quint Cities region. The pool of resources available each grant cycle is finite, and the best urban & regional planning must craft the hard skills that must be learned.

Learning how grant funding is disbursed and who receives what and how much is crucial. Every recipient is an element of the mosaic of our Quint

Cities region. Focusing on one single nonprofit group never lets you see the grant mosaic. However, if you peruse the list of the 2022 grant cycle recipients and see all the recipients as one giant mosaic, then you can understand how each nonprofit is helping shape the perspectives of area residents and the perceptions of the rest of our nation and in the international community.

Chapter XXV

IQCF [DEI] Research 2023

      The IQCF mission we are developing is a diverse, inclusive Quint Cities region. The IQCF volunteers researched dozens of live concerts in the Quint Cities region since August 2021. The IQCF precursor, the International Tastemaker Fest Thesis, documented hundreds of live performances in the QC since 2014. The purpose of researching our live music scene is learning how our audience interacts with the talent we draw from other regions of our nation and the world. We then apply our observations of the live music scene and develop diversity, cultural equity, inclusion, talent attraction, and arts & cultural sustainability. We are specifically researching the coming multiethnic majority audience emerging in the QC.

November 5th, 2021, the IQCF volunteers enjoyed several bands at the Raccoon Motel including Road Soda, the Many-Colored Death and, Radkey. Road Soda is a local QC punk band with a rabid following. The sound is fast, loud, and imminently punk. Road Soda is like the Ramones and Motorhead enjoying brunch at Perkins. "…The overall angle is one of fun, not brutality. Clearly these guys have a sense of humor and are poking fun at punk traditions as much as honoring them."[xxxix] Further, Road Soda are fixtures on the local Quad Cities music scene. You will see members of Road Soda at lots of local concerts in the Quad Cities supporting other bands.

The Many-Colored Death rocked the stage after Road Soda. The three piece is hard and tight prog grunge like Rush and Soundgarden grew up with each other at a boarding school in Wales. [Brent] "…Moore, bassist Preston Rodgers and drummer Shea Spence complement each other, pulling their share of the rock 'n' roll load and creating a sound that honors rock gods like Rush, Pink Floyd and Soundgarden while establishing its own distinct personality."[xl] The band is really tight, and all the songs are well rehearsed. The gear is professionally designed, and the sound is one of a kind.

Headliners, Radkey, were truly rad. The power punk trio of the brothers Radke, Isaiah, Solomon, and Dee [bass, drums, guitar] are a punk rock band with chops. You can hear the Ramones and Green Day, however, Radkey crafts a unique punk rock sound that is their own. "Whatever their influences, Radkey evade the mistake of dipping into the empty…[riffage]…of acts like <u>Greta Van Fleet</u>. But I also won't call them "modern". Radkey play rock (or in their words, "delicious rock noise"). The timeless elements heard throughout *Green Room*…see Radkey poised…for future growth, and you can bet that Radkey will rise and meet the challenge….[xli] We observe the Radkey stage presence could be at any large festival ala Coachella, Lollapalooza, etc. Keep your ears peeled.

November 11th, 2021, the IQCF volunteers enjoyed the spectacular talents of Carver Commodores and Whitehall at the Raccoon Motel. South Carolina band Whitehall is cool indie emo, like the early Shins. The band is tight, and despite the departure of the original saxophone player, Whitehall continues making new music and touring.[xlii] The sound is like Houndmouth and Weezer made a band with Petey. Whitehall is certainly a crowd favorite at the Raccoon Motel.

Keep your ears peeled because Whitehall is making waves.

        Carver Commodore was the headliner, and this is a cool band, perhaps your new favorite band. "After releasing their debut album in 2017, Florence-based band has consistently won over audiences with their style of rock and roll that blends the sound of the early 21st century garage rock bands (think The Strokes and The White Stripes) with the soulful voice of lead singer Payton Pruitt that pulls listeners into their music headfirst."[xliii] The new Carver Commodore album *"Welcome to the Modern World,"* is way cool. The band nails every track on the album and is one of the best live bands I seen/heard in a long time. We highly recommend following Carver Commodore and the raucous live show of the new band from the Florence side of Muscle Shoals, Alabama.

        December 11th, 2021, we enjoyed the wonderful Elizabeth Moen at the Raccoon Motel. Elizabeth Moen, an Iowa native from Vinton is a self-taught guitarist and singer-songwriter. Her voice is like Billie Holiday and Nina Simone joined a club with Bonnie Raitt. The sound is almost bluesy, but veers away from cliché'. We always enjoy when Elizabeth Moen is in the Quad Cities. Elizabeth "…emerge[d] within the…[Iowa City]… musical scene while completing her undergraduate degree at the University of Iowa. …[T]he transition to writing her own songs and lyrics, and how intimate and locally owned music venues are essential to newly developing artists…"[xliv] is evident when we see Elizabeth on stage at the Raccoon Motel here in the Quad Cities.

December 19th, 2021, the IQCF volunteers heard the spectacular Zella Day with special guest Jesse Woods at the Raccoon Motel. Zella Day is original in a real sense. Her sound is ethereal acoustic space folk. Her lyrics are quite intelligent and make you wonder from whence her song ideas come. "West Coast-raised,…Zella has composed music just shy of 20 years…. By 20-years-old, her first album brought her performances at Coachella, Bonnaroo, TV appearances, and a[n] ever-expanding fan base…. [Zella]…found her place in a tight knit community of artists including Lana Del Rey, Weyes Blood and, BORNS. [Zella]…produced an EP with Dan Auerbach and appeared on Lana Del Rey's record, *Chemtrails Over the Country Club*. And now, she's ready to add another accolade to her blossoming portfolio…"[xlv] her new album *Where Does the Devil Hide?* Accompanying Zella on electric guitar was the reflective artistry of Jesse Woods. Jesse Woods is an artist in his own right. His sound, like Zella, is "…hazy neo-folk…."[xlvi] The collaboration between Zella and Jesse is natural and they might compose songs with each other someday. We highly recommend you peruse the sounds of Zella Day.

January 28th, 2022, the IQCF volunteers heard Matthew Logan Vasquez[xlvii] and Warmtapes at the Raccoon Motel. Warmtapes is a singer-songwriter from Houston, Texas with incredible compositions skills and vocal chops.[xlviii] The songs are indie/alternative on the acoustic guitar rather than folk, or countrified indie rock. The songs are clever love, heartache, and longing themes. Certainly, Warmtapes will garner a loyal following from the subjects and themes, as well as his adept musical skills.

Matthew Logan Vasquez and his band were the headliners. Matthew Logan Vasquez of Delta Spirit fame is a cool band leader and the MLV songs are all well written. The chemistry of his band on stage is palpable and the songs make you smile. The success of Delta Spirit is officially "on hiatus," however, the songwriting skills of MLV are as strong as they ever were. The subject matter of the MLV songs is unique. "…Vazquez says that his own writing is rarely random, and that he…[seeks cerebral themes]…. 'I don't just write songs about love and breakups,' he maintains. 'I write songs about life and death, small stuff…. I just wrote a song about Jane Pauley. She's so cool! I can't wait for people to hear that one.'"[xlix] The public usually thinks all songs are autobiographical, however, MLV reveals that some songs are fiction. Deciding what is autobiographical and fiction makes the listening an interesting experience.

February 5th, 2022, the IQCF volunteers were present at the Darryl Rahn, and Taylor Goldsmith acoustic sets at the Raccoon Motel. Darryl Rahn is like James Taylor joined Simon & Garfunkel. The sound is folkish with apt finger work on the fret board that remains acoustic folk throughout his acoustic set. His songs are somewhat autobiographical. Regarding the songs from his Raccoon Motel set, Rahn says "…'This set of songs is very story-driven and detail-oriented. Usually, I aim to write about other people, but these are almost all inspired by my life.'"[l] The stage banter at the Raccoon Motel was full of chuckles from Rahns' story telling between songs. Rahn relayed a story of writing songs in a hotel room on tour. Rahn said he heard a couple having sex in the next room while he was practicing and he couldn't decide if they were moaning because they liked his songs, or because they wanted Rahn to quit playing. The crowd laughed.

Taylor Goldsmith was the headliner and the crowd favorite. Taylor Goldsmith is the lead singer-songwriter from the band Dawes. The entertainment value of Taylor Goldsmith is immense. The lyrics are like a wise storyteller speaking with the audience sometimes in a whisper. Taylor describes his lyrical approach explaining "…why a guy like Warren Zevon is maybe [Taylors'] favorite lyricist, because it's always smart. …complicated ideas. [Warren] is…creating complicated reactions from a listener. But you never are misunderstanding what he's getting after."[li] The insights of how singer-songwriters produce lyrics is always interesting. Lyrics might be autobiographical or mere fiction. Taylor Goldsmith is comfortable on stage, and you can see and hear the years of practice. The future is bright regarding Taylor Goldsmith, Dawes and whatever future projects might occur. We highly recommend giving Taylor Goldsmith and Dawes a listen.

February 12th, 2022, the stellar volunteers of the IQCF enjoyed a wonderful night of music at the Racccoon Motel. Local favorite Angela Meyer was the lead in for the world-famous BJ Barnham[lii]. The sound of BJ Barnham is alt-country. Part Hank Williams, part Honky Tonk, and just a splash of southern twang. The sound is cool, and we encourage you should explore the ideas of the lyrics of BJ Barham.

March 4ᵗʰ, 2022, the night was the "local bash" at the Raccoon Motel. Johnnie Cluney, local favorites Tambourine and, Gary J & the Pancake Brothers. Johnnie Cluney. Johnnie Cluney is an **illustrator and musician from Illinois**. He has done all the artist illustrations for the Daytrotter sessions. His sound is cool psychedelia with an electric guitar and whammy bar. Tambourine[liii] was next up and band leader Chad Gooch from Moline is a prolific songwriter. The songs are vintage 1990s indie rock ala Husker Du, etc. The closing act was Gary J & the Pancake Brothers. The band are really local favorites Mountain Swallower[liv] performing under an assumed band name. The sound of the Pancake Brothers is seriously cool, and they could become huge someday. We recommend you review all these artists and purchase music and merchandise.

March 18ᵗʰ, 2022, the IQCF volunteers enjoyed a cool night of music at the Raccoon Motel. Izzy Heltai[lv] was the first act and the headliner was Liza Anne. Liza Anne has long been a vocal proponent of mental health and wellness, and she has been taking action on that passion outside of her music too. During the pandemic, she's hosted an Instagram Live series on Tuesday evenings titled #EmotionalHealth2020. In each episode, she speaks with another friend or collaborator (Mancari,

Caroline Rose and Shamir have been past guests) about how they care for themselves emotionally.[lvi] The sound of Liza Anne is like David Bowie space odyssey mixed with PJ Harvey and a dash of Joan Jett. We believe you should review these artists and hear the sounds, lyrics, and ideas behind the music.

March 29th, 2022, the IQCF volunteers were on site at the Raccoon Motel enjoying the sounds of Willy Mason[lvii] with local fixture Angela Meyer as the first act. His sound is unique with an acoustic guitar, vocals and a strange electric guitar pick up linked with a ¼" cable. The electric guitar pick up is then placed in a hardcover book which Willy puts on the floor and thumps with is foot as the rhythm section. Regarding the inspiration of his songs, Willy will tell you best. "I think the biggest thing was that there was this girl I decided I wanted to make a mixtape for, and to do that I had to set up a bunch of equipment because I wanted to dub some vinyl. So, I started dusting things off and plugging things in and I got carried away and started making music to put onto the mixtape. It started with interludes in-between the songs and then it just kind of went from there. So, the first iteration of this album was…on a tape."[lviii] We encourage you enjoy the sounds of Willy Mason.

April 7th, 2022, the IQCF volunteers discovered some new talents. Grumpy was the first act followed by Hotel Fiction with Susto as the headliner. Grumpy[lix] is a cool band with awesome songs. We encourage you research and enjoy the sounds of Grumpy. Hotel Fiction[lx] are a really cool band with female lead singers. The inception of Hotel Fiction was pure happenstance. Jade Long and Jessica Thompson knew there was magic in the air when they started writing songs together in 2018. After meeting at the University of Georgia through mutual friends with whom they had jam sessions, Long and Thompson began meeting every Friday.[lxi] We encourage you enjoy the sounds of Hotel Fiction.

      May 13th, 2022, the IQCF volunteers enjoyed a night of heavy metal at the Raccoon Motel. The first act was the Central and the headliner was Everlasting Light.[lxii] Rock Island-based black-metal band Everlasting Light has been a favorite Quad Cities project of mine since the release of *Heavy Sanctuary* back in 2019. A project that revels in the extra layer of obfuscating scuzz that comes from a more informal approach to recording, they still always manage to hit a sweet spot between the high-fidelity detail of a "proper" studio take and the more room-tone-soaked final product of a DIY demo tape.[lxiii] The Central[lxiv] was the first act and are a really heavy band. We encourage you enjoy these bands and if you like heavy metal, you will really enjoy these bands.

July 9th, 2022, the IQCF volunteers were on site at the Racoon Motel enjoying the sounds of Elizabeth Moen[lxv].   Regarding the composition style of Elizabeth Moen, the artist will tell you in her own words. "Honestly, I've been creating more than I think I ever was," Moen admitted. Moen, who began writing songs during her senior year of college, said her creative practice was much shorter and more sporadic in the past. She would often sit down to write a few songs, then jump into performing them live, spending little time refining the material. Live music was the focal point of her artistic experience. When that had to stop, more or less, for the last two years, she leaned into the more technical aspects of her craft, from learning new instruments to embracing collaborations with other artists."[lxvi]

These are just a few of the bands we researched in 2021 while planning the inaugural IQCF July 30th, 2022. We will certainly be researching lots of bands all year long between the annual IQCF. Our mission is drawing talent from other regions and building a diverse, inclusive Quint Cities region. Music is a language that can be one of the best instruments of change when developing urban & regional planning. Designing new complex systems with cultural sustainability in arts and culture is an element of the IQCF mission.

Chapter XXVI

*Diversity, Cultural Equity &
Inclusion 2022*

We learned the elements diversity, equity &
inclusion [DEI] in terms of Corporate Social
Responsibility [CSR] in the IQCF 2022 publishing.
This year we will research diversity, equity &
inclusion in arts and culture. Further, we will get at
the root causes of the irresponsible wealth gap in
our nation. We learned race-baiting is the red
herring that deflects attention away from the origins
of the wealth gap, cycle of poverty and systemic
racism. Race-baiting is a trite strategy and never
solves origins of the wealth gap, cycle of poverty
and systemic racism we see in our nation.

However, our emerging multiethnic audience is getting at the root of the origins of the wealth gap. Poverty is color blind.

Non-minority Americans must realize systemic racism is an ill effect of the unequal access of wealth and resources. Proper diversity, cultural equity & inclusion planning in our communities must be cognizant of the wealth gap first. Integration of races is becoming natural, and the social friction racial integration causes is a product of the wealth gap. The modern wealth gap is the result of post-Civil War 14th Amendment era laws and inefficient complex systems causing systemic racism. Systemic racism is becoming a relic of the past every day as our nation is becoming a multiethnic majority. Cultural equity is the part of the diversity, cultural equity & inclusion models we must research.

Equality means every individual obtains the same resources regardless of socioeconomic status. Cultural equity is the idea that underserved populations should receive resources that provide equal access of resources. All humans are equal, however, lack of access of resources is why cultural equity is a crucial element of the diversity, equity, and inclusion equation. Urban & regional planners must realize that redesigning new, modern complex systems must include developing cultural equity and environmental sustainability.

Developing cultural equity is the challenging part of diversity, cultural equity, and inclusion models. The population is diverse, and inclusion is codified in law since the 1960s. However, cultural equity is somewhat elusive because providing access of resources is a quagmire of inefficient organization and administration. Every community in our nation and the world develops programs in line with the local demographics. We learned the practice of gerrymandering and the effect of redistricting and that affects cultural equity and access of resources in what appears an inefficient design on purpose.

Gerrymandering and redistricting exclude certain neighborhoods from voting districts, and that might dilute the voice of a perceived "popular vote." Watch dog groups follow gerrymandering practices and sound the alarm when a voting district appears gerrymandered. The Supreme Court of every state in the nation hears arguments against the gerrymandering of voting districts almost every year. Is gerrymandering of voting districts a sign of the wealth gap, cycle of poverty and systemic racism? These are the tough questions we will answer herein.

Laws are changing and cultural equity is becoming the vehicle of socioeconomic change. Arguments exist regarding cultural equity because redistribution of wealth is a hot issue. The redistribution of wealth is a challenge because redistribution of wealth won't solve the wealth gap, cycle of poverty, or address the scourge of systemic racism. We must maintain a minimum social safety net in our nation. However, are social safety net programs ending the wealth gap, cycle of poverty and systemic racism?

Intelligent design of new complex systems that embrace diversity, cultural equity and inclusion will help end both the vicious cycle of poverty and systemic racism. The challenge is the connection between poverty and race which always appears elusive because poverty is color blind. We learned public school funding is a state right because of the language of the 14th Amendment of the US Constitution. The 14th Amendment era laws are a relic of post-Civil War lawmakers. The states argued that public education is a state right and states can decide how they fund their public schools. If every individual is guaranteed a free public education, then states decided public schools would be funded with property tax. That is why public schools remain funded with property taxes and why barriers exist at low-income school districts. We can and must redesign how public schools are funded. Laws change every day. Public school funding is a product of the inefficient complex systems that preserved the wealth gap.

Proper design of cultural equity initiatives ensures our underserved populations experiencing the cycle of poverty obtain access of resources. Equal access of resources alone won't solve either the wealth gap, cycle of poverty, or systemic racism in our nation. Cultural equity is a vehicle of change that empowers underserved populations with the skills required in obtaining and accumulating generational wealth. Closing the wealth gap must include cultural equity in the diversity, cultural equity, and inclusion equation.

Social service programs are getting better every year and laws are always changing. Our nation is wealthiest nation on Earth and every individual deserves the chance at obtaining and accumulating generational wealth. However, cultural equity barriers prevent individuals experiencing the wealth gap, cycle of poverty and/or systemic racism from closing the wealth gap. We will research socioeconomic and political barriers in Chapter VII and Chapter VIII. Certainly, America as a nation was and is built with labor, however, we must realize labor must receive wages. The legacy of our nation must embrace modern diversity, cultural equity, and inclusion when urban & regional planning. Social unrest and other ills will be a relic of the past when every individual is raised in an environment that is the natural progression of modern socioeconomic and political complex systems. Inefficient complex systems of the past that caused the wealth gap, cycle of poverty and systemic racism will be and are being dismantled.

Chapter XXVII

The IQCF 2023

The second annual IQCF is on July 29th, 2023, in the Quint Cities. The inaugural IQCF was a smashing success, and the first annual IQCF food drive was wonderful. We are planning new venues, films, and culinary talents in 2023. This year we are developing our diversity, cultural equity and inclusion initiatives and designing new complex systems that help end the wealth gap, cycle of poverty and systemic racism. The talents we are drawing here will be an integral part of building new, modern complex systems in the Quad Cities. Raising awareness of ending the wealth gap, cycle of poverty and systemic racism is an element of the IQCF mission. The question is how arts, culture & heritage can further the causes of our underserved populations?

Arts, culture & heritage can further the causes of our underserved populations in a myriad of ways. Creative placemaking is one vehicle we can employ in the integration of all races and social classes. First, we must thoroughly research the demographics of the Quad Cities and identify the underserved populations who lack access of arts, culture & heritage because of socioeconomic barriers. We must dismantle barriers that prevent individuals experiencing the vicious cycle of poverty from enjoying the same access of arts and culture individuals experiencing the cycle of wealth enjoy. Dismantling cultural equity barriers will help end the wealth gap, cycle of poverty and systemic racism.

We learned in the preceding IQCF publications that the demographics of the Quad Cities are quite diverse. The Blackhawk Tribe, other local tribes, African Americans, Irish, German, Sweden, Indian, West African, Asian and virtually every nationality on the planet resides here in the QC. We must be cognizant of the wealth of diverse cultures and develop an urban and regional planning approach that integrates our wealth of diverse cultures. The most recent US Census reveals our nation will soon be a multiethnic majority. Planning the IQCF will be a world model of effective integration of all cultures.

Arts and culture organizations must realize new audiences are emerging and a new world culture is becoming a multiethnic audience. Community partnerships are a crucial element of developing a new multiethnic audience here in the QC. Azubuike African American Arts is a nonprofit making films of African American culture here in the QC. The producers, filmmakers, actors and actresses, and support staff are all African Americans. Azubuike is providing African American artists with access of the means of arts, culture, and filmmaking production with large grants from the Moline Foundation and the QC Community Foundation. The IQCF will be building partnerships with Azubuike, and we believe we can bridge the gap between all cultures here in the QC with partnerships like Azubuike.

The key is providing access of arts and culture our multiethnic population might never obtain otherwise. Obtaining access of arts and culture is a process of partnerships and collaborations within the community of nonprofit organizations in the QC. Providing access of arts and culture is a sign that systemic barriers are being dismantled. Change is generational and we can provide our future generations with the foundation. The local grant making foundations disperse millions of dollars every year. Providing our marginalized populations with access of the grant funding is an element of the IQCF mission.

This year's IQCF will build on the foundation of the International Quint Cities Festival, the IQCF 2022 publishings and the inaugural IQCF. The QC is becoming more diverse and multiethnic every day. We must be prepared and give the new emerging multiethnic audience access of arts and culture. Arts and culture are a vehicle of cultural integration. Futurism teaches us that someday all humans will be the same color and speak the same language. Art and culture are a universal language and that is why arts and culture will be a leader in developing our new, modern complex systems and emerging multiethnic audience.

Our diversity, cultural equity and inclusion plan this year will employ all models of socioeconomic urban & regional planning. We see progress with changing laws and the wealth gap is somewhat being addressed in a modern way with new modern programs. The grants mosaic of the Quad Cities is a resource you can research and employ when building diversity, cultural equity, and inclusion. Philanthropy in the QC will advance the mission of the IQCF in providing access of arts and culture. Raising awareness of unequal access of resources is crucial.

Remember what we are learning regarding public school funding and the wealth gap. Public school funding models are codified in law since the 14th Amendment state rights debate in the US Congress. Public schools are funded with property tax and the neighborhoods with the highest property tax build the largest public schools with the best equipment and facilities. Neighborhoods with lowest property tax see substandard school equipment and facilities. Substandard public school equipment and facilities are cultural equity barriers we must dismantle. One element of the IQCF mission is raising awareness of the cultural equity barriers that prevent low-income school districts from accessing equal school equipment and facilities.

The URTEs [urban renewal tax exemption] zones in Davenport help us learn how urban & regional planners are addressing the lack of per pupil funding. Lack of per pupil funding is a hot issue in the Davenport Quad Cities. Remember, public school funding comes from property taxes, a relic of the 14th Amendment states' rights laws. We must redesign our public school funding models. However, public school funding is a fierce debate in every state legislature and such changes are slow. School vouchers, charter schools, private schools, etc. are signs that wealthy populations want education that is non-traditional and are leaving the public school system. However, public schools are just as good as private schools.

Every year the IQCF will raise awareness with our mission. Providing our underserved populations with access of arts and culture will change the cultural interaction and build our multiethnic audience. That might sound like small change, however, access of arts and culture, like access of public school funding are signals that inefficiently designed complex systems are changing. Urban & regional planning isn't one single individual's job. Urban & regional planning is the job of every individual in every town in every nation.

Chapter XXVIII

New Films & Venues

The IQCF is building on *the International Tastemaker Fest Thesis* regarding developing a new international town each year. Thus far we developed the QC, Dublin, Hamburg, Barcelona, London, Reykjavik, Iceland and in 2023 we are developing Glasgow, Scotland. The IQCF global brand becoming established. The new venue we are developing and the new films we are developing in the 2023 festival are an awesome addition with the films we researched in *the International Tastemaker Fest Thesis* and *the International Quint Cities Festival*. See the list of new films below.

1945

https://www.menemshafilms.com
https://www.katapultfilm.hu
https://www.theguardian.com/film/2018/oct/12/1945-review-
ferenc-torok-holocaust-second-world-war

"On a summer day in 1945, an Orthodox man and his grown son return to a village in Hungary while the villagers prepare for the wedding of the town clerk's son. The townspeople – suspicious, remorseful, fearful, and cunning – expect the worst and behave accordingly. The town clerk fears the men may be heirs of the village's deported Jews and expects them to demand their illegally acquired property back.

Director Ferenc Török paints a complex picture of a society trying to come to terms with the recent horrors they've experienced, perpetrated, or just tolerated for personal gain. A superb ensemble cast, lustrous black and white cinematography, and historically detailed art direction contribute to an eloquent drama that reiterates Thomas Wolfe's famed sentiment: you can't go home again."[lxvii]

65

www.beckwoods.com
https://www.bleedingcool.com/movies/65-actor-
adam-driver-to-star-in-sam-raimi-produced-sony-
sci-fi-film/

Adam

Charlotte

"Elegant animation and all-star voices…tell the story of a German-Jewish painter who left an extraordinary body of work before her untimely death. …Charlotte Salomon (Keira Knightly voice) comes of age as the Nazis rise to power. Forced from a famed Berlin art academy amid growing anti-Semitism, she escapes to the South of France. Defying her tragic family lineage and looming dangers, Charlotte experiences an awakening, …romance and painting…"[lxviii]

Eyimofe

Jews of the Wild West

"[T]he…contributions of Jews on the American frontier are…researched. Escaping oppression and poverty, Jewish families joined other…Americans and European immigrations in search of a better life. …100,000 Jews put roots in the Wild West, from Guggenheim and Levi Strauss and everyday merchants and cattlemen. …Interviews and…archival research recalls the legacy of Jews who shaped westward expansion."[lxix]

https://www.jewsofthewildwest.com/
https://ajff.org/film/jews-wild-west

Leeches

https://www.zillionfilm.com

Leona

https://www.menemshafilms.com

Merry Christmas, Yiwu

https://www.bocalupofilms.com

Movements

https://www.jeondahee.com

Salam

https://www.salaudmorisset.com

The Auschwitz Report

https://www.israelifilms.co.il
https://www.atlantajewishtimes.timesofisrae
l.com/ajff-intro-the-auschwitz-report/

"This is the true story of Freddy and Walter-
-two young Slovak Jews, who were deported to
Auschwitz in 1942. On 10 April 1944, after
meticulous planning, and with the help and
resilience of their inmates, they manage to escape.
While the inmates they had left behind,
courageously stand their ground against Nazi
officers, the two men are driven on by the hope that
their evidence can save lives. Emaciated and hurt,
they make their way through the mountains…and
enter…Slovakia. With the help of chance
encounters, they…cross the border and meet the
resistance, and...international assistance agencies….

They…[preserve]…a detailed report about the systematic genocide at the camp…. Nazi propaganda and international liaisons…were…still in place, however,…and their tale sounds unbelievable….[lxx]

The Cemil Show
https://www.alphaviolet.com

The Cotton Wool War
https://www.imdb.com

The French Dispatch
https://www.searchlightpictures.com/thefrenchdispatch
https://www.variety.com/2021/film/news/wes-anderson-french-dispatch-release-date-2-1234982978/

The Planters
https://www.theplanters.com
https://www.hollywoodreporter.com/review/planters-afi-2019-1255610

We encourage you view all the films we researched since *the International Tastemaker Fest Thesis* and *the International Quint Cities Festival* publishings.

The films here are merely additions on the lengthy list we established in the previous Executive Producers' publishings. The films help shape our perceptions and perspectives and speak an international language on the world stage. The power of film imagery is immense. We believe our lengthy list of films is unique of our festival. Every film festival curates a list of films, and our list of films is in line with our mission of developing a diverse, inclusive Quint Cities region and building sustainable cultural equity and environmental preservation.

Chapter XXIX

War on Poverty Changes

The War on Poverty is ever changing. We are learning the complex systems that cause and nourish the cycle of poverty. Raising awareness of the systemic causes of the cycle of poverty will help end socioeconomic and sociopolitical unrest throughout the world. Developing new complex systems with our diversity, cultural equity and inclusion research will help end the scourge of systemic racism and provide future generations with a natural environment of inclusion.

We learned the idea that our social safety net [SNAP, WIC, TANF] is a design that never addresses the underlying causes of the wealth gap, cycle of poverty and systemic racism. Individuals experiencing the cycle of poverty are usually unaware of the origins of the wealth gap, cycle of poverty and systemic racism. The systemic causes of poverty are rooted in our nation's history. Modern urban & regional planners must design new complex systems that raise awareness of diversity, cultural equity, and inclusion. The truth is expecting our population should understand complex systems is unrealistic.

The expectation that individuals experiencing the cycle of poverty should understand the systemic causes of the cycle of poverty is unrealistic because lack of access of resources shapes the world view of individuals in the cycle of poverty. However, ending systemic racism is the natural progression of our nation and the new world. The socioeconomic and political strife of the past will be ancient history. Futurism is becoming a new school of thought. Predicting the future was an ancient art and modern futurism is becoming a science.

Leaders emerge and make changes; however, changes will come faster if our nation redesigns new, modern complex systems providing access of resources employing new models of diversity, cultural equity, and inclusion. One single individual in our nation and the world at large should ever espouse a world view with built in barriers. The future will be natural and every individual on the planet will be raised never experiencing the systemic cycle of poverty. Certainly, the new world view will be generational. However, each new generation will enjoy the ever-changing complex systems that end the cycle of poverty, and the plague of systemic racism will be ancient history.

Race-baiting is the red herring that causes cultural quagmires and ineffective debates with the world population. Raising awareness of the wealth gap will help future generations end the wealth gap, cycle of poverty, systemic racism and, embrace the new world multiethnic audience. The days of lack of access of capital and resources will be over. New generations will learn of the relics of our nation and the worlds past with new public school funding models and never experience inefficient complex systems that caused the wealth gap, cycle of poverty and systemic racism.

Arts and culture are an element of bridging the wealth gap from every race and social class. Ending the war on poverty must be a combination of local, regional, national, and international organizations, foundations, and individuals. Like the oil of diplomacy in politics, arts and culture are the oil of cultural diplomacy easing the friction of cultural integration of all races and social classes.

Arts and culture are somewhat of a universal language. If we encourage arts and culture, then different languages and cultures can speak a universal language and design new, intelligent complex systems.

New complex systems are ending the socioeconomic, political, and cultural equity barriers that cause the wealth gap, cycle of poverty and systemic racism. Inefficient complex systems since the 14th Amendment era lawmakers built the wealth gap, cycle of poverty and the tragedy of systemic racism. Diligent research and intelligent urban & regional planning can and must develop new modern complex systems that end the wealth gap, cycle of poverty, systemic racism and reflect our emerging multiethnic majority audience.

The lessons of the pandemic were a moment when public school funding became a national issue. Parents want school vouchers in exchange of the funds state governments employ with public schools. The schools with the highest property tax receive the highest per pupil funding. Public schools are funded with property tax, and we must redesign public school funding models that address school districts with the lowest property tax. The previous Superintendent of the Davenport School District was censured from the State of Iowa Board of Education because of his protest against unequal per pupil funding in the Davenport School District. The protest was symbolic and appeared ineffective after the censure. However, the protest was an element of the mosaic public school funding protests we see in every state of the nation. Public funding models will change.

Here we are getting at the root of the wealth gap, cycle of poverty and systemic racism. The post-Civil War lawmakers in the US Congress designed the 14th Amendment of the US Constitution as a compromise [was that really a compromise or a clue of the origin of the wealth gap, cycle of poverty and systemic racism?] and therein states that whatever issue isn't mentioned in the US Constitution becomes a state right. Public school funding became and remains a state right. The 14th Amendment era lawmakers of each state then decided that, since public school funding is a state right, then each state decided public schools would be funded with property tax. What segment of the population owned the most property post-Civil War? These are the tough questions that raise awareness of the origins of the wealth gap in our nation. Research suggests that most of the population is unaware of the wealth gap. That will change with the new modern complex systems we are designing.

The debate is fierce regarding public school funding. The lowest property tax school districts might include the top sports and scholarly talents; however, lack of adequate equipment and facilities is what are called barriers. Diversity, cultural equity, and inclusion models want all barriers dismantled. The dismantling of barriers in our public schools must first change the current models of public school funding and design new, modern public school funding models. We can then let the public school funding models established with the 14th Amendment rest in the dust bin of ancient history.

Chapter XXX

Sustainability Research 2023

We researched sustainability regarding CSR [Corporate Social Responsibility] with the annual IQCF 2022 publishing. This year we will build on our sustainability research and apply the ideas with arts and culture. CSR, arts, culture, and the environment are emerging as leaders in cultural and environmental sustainability programs. Again, the task with cultural and environmental sustainability is learning the best practices of changing inefficient complex systems and building the best future.

Environmental preservation is a mainstream popular culture movement. Cultural sustainability and environmental preservation are good friends. I agree we must preserve and protect the planet. However, we must raise awareness of the wealth gap, cycle of poverty and systemic racism caused from inefficient complex systems first. Sustainable environmental preservation is the natural result of ending the cycle of poverty and systemic racism. Getting at the "…root causes…and…[designing new complex systems]…we must realize…environmental preservation…are intertwined with socioeconomic cycles.…Low-income communities and communities of color are affected the most because low-income populations are more likely to have toxic industries in their neighborhoods and more vulnerable to the effects of climate change."[lxxi]

Regarding sustainability in arts and culture, there are lots of buzz words like "creative placemaking." "Creative placemaking is a kind of artistic practice that engages directly with and in geographically defined communities to make change."[lxxii] The IQCF mission likes the idea of creative placemaking. The IQCF volunteers are researching the best practices of redevelopment of our marginalized groups and will provide access of arts and culture that might never occur otherwise.

Chapter XXXI

Talent Attraction & Ambition

The Quad Cities urban & regional planning groups are developing plans on attracting talent with ambition. The Quad Cities region certainly an attractive region on the Mississippi River. The challenge is attracting talents that might otherwise accept higher salaries in large urban centers. Arts and culture are a key element in attracting talents. Creative placemaking will help make our region a destination. Live music is a good start. The IQCF mission will help draw talents here who might never perform here otherwise.

Live music is just one element of creative placemaking. Researching talent attraction ideas from international towns is a good start. "...*The Mastering of a Music City*...researches...global cities where an understanding exists that arts, culture, and music specifically, help to attract talent and business. Fredrik Sandsten, Event Manager Music at the public tourism agency in Sweden says of Gothenburg, 'We...are...a very industrial city with huge industrial companies. They want culture and music to flourish because they see the link to attracting young workers to their companies.'"[lxxiii] Our local grant making foundations are helping arts and culture groups develop our live music scene in the QC. The funding our arts and culture groups receive help develop festivals, events, films, and venues.

Like the Viper Room and Mojo in Hamburg, developing a venue that is a local brand helps put our region on the map and attracts talents from afar. Almost every large town develops a talent attraction plan and arts, culture and music are a huge element. Gothenburg, Sweden is a large industrial town and attracts talent with the flourishing arts, culture, and music scene. The QC is a farm economy; however, we employ thousands of individuals at our several large industries including the new Amazon facility in Davenport.

Regardless of the nature of a towns industry, if industry and employment are there, then talent attraction and retention must be diligently planned. The idea is the individuals employed in the QC should patronize the local businesses. Arts and culture groups must develop a vibrant local culture that encourages reinvestment of labor earnings with our local businesses rather than leave and patronize businesses elsewhere. Further, the vibrant local culture will attract talent from other regions, increase our population, and build a premier regional destination.

Chapter XXXII

Planning IQCF 2024

The IQCF 2024 will build on the progress of
IQCF 2022 and 2023. The building process
includes our marginalized populations first. New
ideas are almost always met with skepticism and
resistance. That is a sign the idea might be good.
Regardless, the IQCF mission is clear. The research
is sound and valid. Rather than argue the ideas, we
developed an IQCF email and business line at our
new website www.internationalqcf.org and
encourage suggestions. If other multicultural,
multiethnic nonprofit groups, individuals,

foundations, or organizations propose ideas, then the IQCF volunteers will certainly help.

Meanwhile, we must build on the progress thus far. The inaugural IQCF year was a smashing success. We obtained grant funding, manufactured our IQCF tshirts and stickers at Davenport Printing Co., and collected hundreds of cans of food and received a thank you letter from the Community Center Circle Pantry at 6th and Vine. Regarding the tshirts, the grant funding helped the IQCF provide residents of the homeless shelters, free meal sites and residents of the Hamburg District with free tshirts.

This year the IQCF volunteers will research and attend live performances of artists and musicians at our local venues. The idea of talent attraction and ambition is what we learned in Chapter IX, specifically, the international industrial town of Gothenburg, Sweden. If our local business groups and grant making foundations want talent attraction, then we must diligently build our local music, arts, and culture scene. Research is clear that talent attraction and retention is highest in towns with a vibrant music, arts, and culture scene.

We researched Elon Musk and AOC in the IQCF 2022 publishing, and we are seeing lots of changes since that publishing. The space race is becoming huge, and the colonization of Mars is within sight. AOCs crusade against the rich somewhat stalled in a quagmire because the scope of the idea was misguided. However, what is clear is the wealth gap in our nation exists. The IQCF publishing's are getting at the root cause of the wealth gap. AOCs "tax the rich" idea is misguided because how can we be sure the extra tax revenue will be employed in ending the inefficient complex systems that caused the wealth gap in the first place? Social safety net programs deflect attention from the cause of the wealth gap, cycle of poverty and systemic racism seemingly on purpose.

Elon Musk and the space race is some of the best futurism science. However, when we colonize Mars, will humans establish inefficient complex systems on Mars that cause the wealth gap, cycle of poverty and systemic racism like here on Earth? The best future on whatever planet must design new, modern complex systems that end the wealth gap, cycle of poverty and systemic racism. Dismantling the wealth gap, cycle of poverty and systemic racism here on Earth is occurring at the moment. Small law changes here and there is the sign the inefficient complex systems causing the wealth gap, cycle of poverty and systemic racism are being dismantled.

Famine, food insecurity, housing insecurity, homelessness is irresponsible with such vast wealth on planet Earth. We can and must change the inefficient complex systems and dismantle the wealth gap, cycle of poverty and systemic racism first. The colonization of Mars is a new chance at designing the best socioeconomic and political systems humankind ever saw. However, the changes can and must occur here on Earth first.

Ending the wealth gap means we must research the origins of the wealth gap first, and we are. The IQCF 2023 publishing will give us the skills we can employ in designing better, modern complex systems. Remember, the origins of the modern wealth gap are a relic of the 14th Amendment era lawmakers. We must remember the tough questions from Chapter II. Dismantling the wealth gap involves diligent research of inefficient complex system designs. That is the task we are diligently researching herein. Race-baiting is a trite strategy that deflects attention from the origins of the wealth gap on purpose. Getting at the root of the origin of the wealth gap, cycle of poverty and systemic racism is hard because we must employ several scientific thought models.

Laws change, however, big changes are usually preceded with small law changes first. The small law changes combine and end inefficient laws that were designed post-Civil War. Public school funding arguments are one of several arguments that are a clue of the origin of the wealth gap, cycle of poverty and systemic racism. The frustration of individuals experiencing ill effects of the wealth gap must be strong and research the origins of the wealth gap herein. Poverty is color blind and if we embrace the coming multiethnic majority audience, we can change the inefficient complex systems that caused the wealth gap in the first place rather than useless debates ending in quagmires.

Regarding the talent attraction plans, the IQCF volunteers will establish friendships with artists and musicians from other regions. Building relationships and friendships with artists and musicians from other regions will help develop a stream of talent here in the QC. Artists and musicians from other regions will be happy with the emerging multiethnic audience here in the QC and put the QC on their tour schedule every year. Meanwhile, all the employees who might otherwise decide on other regions will come here and purchase property and enjoy employment in one of our industries.

The IQCF volunteers will enjoy the learning we obtain from our diligent research of urban &

regional planning. The IQCF volunteers will become our first employees and build their careers in arts, culture, music, and urban & regional planning. That is why the IQCF obtained our EIN [employer identification number] and established our nonprofit corporation. The IQCF inaugural year was a smashing success and established a good foundation that will launch the careers of our IQCF volunteers. Arts, culture and especially the music industry are one of the hardest industries in terms of establishing a career.

This year's IQCF publishing answered the tough questions regarding origins of the wealth gap, cycle of poverty and systemic racism. The IQCF volunteers will build on the research herein and develop ideas of new, modern complex systems that help end the wealth gap, cycle of poverty and systemic racism. All these ideas from a mere arts and culture nonprofit organization. We are employing best practices and building the best future. Remember, always be optimistic. This year will be better than the last.

All proceeds from the sale of the following books support the International Quint Cities Festival tax exempt nonprofit mission of developing a diverse, inclusive Quint Cities region. Purchase of these books is a charitable donation you can deduct for your taxes. Thank you.

Tastemaker Records
Executive Producers Club
The EPC Book

Tastemaker Records
Executive Producers Club
The International Tastemaker Fest Thesis

Tastemaker Records
Executive Producers Club
The International Quint Cities Festival

Tastemaker Records
Executive Producers Club
The IQCF 2022

Tastemaker Records
Executive Producers Club
The Luxembourg Mix

Tastemaker Records
Executive Producers Club
The IQCF 2023

Tastemaker Records
Executive Producers Club
The Gothenburg Mix

Chapter XXXIII

Glossary

Capitalism/Free enterprise: a political and financial system in which the nations' trade and industry are controlled by private owners who earn profit rather than the state.

Communism: a radical political theory derived from Karl Marx that wants class war with the result that all property is publicly owned.

Socialism: a political and financial theory of social organization that wants the means of production, distribution and exchange owned by the community rather than private owners.

The Federal Reserve: the central financial authority of the United States and helps provide the nation with a stable financial system.

Tax shifting: tax shift is a change in taxation that ends or reduces one or several taxes and establishes or increases others while keeping the overall revenue the same.

Urban & regional planning: the technical sociopolitical process involved with the development of and design of land use and the built environment, including air, water, and the infrastructure passing into and out of urban regions, such as communication, transportation, and distribution systems.

References

[i] Buckham, Philip Wentworth, *Theatre of the Greeks*, Cambridge, 1827

[ii] Diogenes Laertius, *Book V, Heraclides*, 92:"And Aristoxenus the musician says, that he composed…dithyrambs…, and inscribed them with the name of Thespis."

[iii]"White Flight Never Ended," Alana Samuels, *The Atlantic,* July 30, 2015.

[iv] *"Bettendorf: A Typical Little German Community",* Arthur Voelliger.

[v] O'Flaherty, Brendan. *City Economics.* Cambridge, Massachusetts. London, England. 2005. Harvard University Press

[vi] "The Influence of Rap/Hip-Hop Music: A Mixed Method Analysis," Gretchen Duffey

[vii] "Rap Music Lost Original Purpose, Materialistic," Jason Swieso

[viii] "Why Big Tobacco Targeted Blacks with Ads for Menthol Cigarettes," Jim Edwards, CBS News, January 6, 2011

[ix] "The Science of Barbie's Effect on Girls Self-Esteem," *Pacific Standard Magazine*, Francie Diep, 1/29/16

[x] "Why This Black Girl Will Not Be Returning to the Women's March," *The Huffington Post*, S.T. Holloway, 1/19/18

[xi] Uzochi P. Nwoko, *The Harvard Crimson*, 4/4/18

[xii] "How Unequal School Funding Punishes Poor Kids," *The Nation*, Michelle Chen 5/11/18]

[xiii] www.planning.org/diversity

[xiv] "Trump Blames Violent Video Games for School Shootings," *Forbes Magazine*, Erik Cain 2/22/18

[xv] www.brookings.edu "New Evidence on School Choice and Racially SegregatedSchools," Grover J. "Russ" Whitehurst 12/14/17]

[xvi] "Gangster Rap and Its Social Cost: Exploiting Hip Hop and Using Racial Stereotypes to Entertain America," Benjamin P. Bowser]

[xvii]

https://cityofdavenportiowa.com/programs_events/grants_programs

[xviii] https://www.scottcountyiowa.com/assessor/exemptions-credits

[xix] http://www.laits.utexas.edu/gov310/PIG/glossary.html
[xx] "How Smaller Cities Are Trying to Plug America's Brain Drain". *Wired, Oberhaus, Daniel 12/8/2019.*
[xxi] "When, Where, and How to Test Market," *Harvard Business Review,* N.D. Cadbury, May 1975
[xxii] "Welfare Offers Short-Term Help and Long-Term Poverty, Thanks to Asset Tests," Jeffrey Dorfman, 10/13/16]
[xxiii] "The Behavioral Aspects of Poverty," www.brookings.edu, Isabell V. Sawhill, 9/1/03.
[xxiv] "Irish and German Immigration," www.khanacademy.org
[xxv] "The Real Lessons from Bill Clinton's Welfare Reform," Vann R. Newkirk II, 2/5/18
[xxvi] "Socialism vs. the Welfare State," PA Times, John Pearson]
[xxvii] "Want to End Poverty? Promote Capitalism, Not Socialism," *Washington Examiner,* Jesse Hathaway, 10/28/18

[xxviii] IRS 1023 research www.foundationgroup.com
[xxix] IRS 1023 document www.irs.gov
[xxx] End Poverty www.borgenproject.org
[xxxi] Farm Aid www.farmaid.org
[xxxii] Nonprofit status, www.grants.gov
[xxxiii] Travel Iowa https://www.traveliowa.com
[xxxiv] Travel Iowa FY2022 grants https://industrypartners.traveliowa.com/iowa-tourism-grants/?
[xxxv] QC Community Foundation, Teens for Tomorrow 2022 grants https://www.qccommunityfoundation.org/news/2022/6/6/pkz84m9nae1bqkavzfoufhk509cy6u
[xxxvi] QC Community Foundation awards $475,000 in local scholarships https://www.qccommunityfoundation.org/news/2022/5/18/local-students-awarded-475000-in-scholarships

[xxxvii] QCCF and Hubbell-Waterman grant $1.2 million to 43 nonprofits https://www.qccommunityfoundation.org/news/2022/3/21/hubbell-waterman-foundation-grants-12-million-to-43-nonprofits
[xxxviii] East Moline Foundation Summer 2022 grant recipients https://www.molinefoundation.org/2022-spring-grant-recipients
[xxxix] Night Freak and Road Soda, https://www.rcreader.com/music/nightfreak-road-soda-oct23

[xl] Five questions with The Many-Colored Death front man Brent Moore, https://www.columbiatribune.com/story/entertainment/2020/11/05/five-questions-many-colored-death-frontman-brent-moore/6085145002/
[xli] Review: Radkeys' 'Green Room' is a rock album for the 21st Century, https://atwoodmagazine.com/radkey-green-room-album-review/
[xlii] South Carolina Band takes 6th Tour and New Projects, http://cravethesound.com/interviews-1/whitehall
[xliii] Catching Up with Carver Commodore, https://masonmusic.com/catching-up-with-carver-commodore/
[xliv] Talking Art with Elizabeth Moen, https://www.wvik.org/2021-08-10/talking-art-with-elizabeth-moen
[xlv] Zella Day | The Retro Sounds of New Indie Pop, https://flaunt.com/content/zella-day
[xlvi] Artist of the Week: Jesse Woods, http://austintownhall.com/tag/jesse-woods/
[xlvii] Checking In: Matthew Logan Vasquez Lives in Parallel Universes, https://www.austinchronicle.com/daily/music/2020-10-27/checking-in-matthew-logan-vasquez-lives-in-parallel-universes/
[xlviii] Chronicle Concerts: Meet indie singer/songwriter Warmtapes from Houston, https://preview.houstonchronicle.com/music/chronicle-concerts-meet-indie-singer-songwriter-15813631
[xlix] True Confessions: Delta Spirits' Matthew Logan Vasquez Talks About Making, Breaking, and Remaking the Band, https://americansongwriter.com/delta-spirit-matthew-logan-interview/
[l] New Hartford-native Darryl Rahn to host live performance to promote 'Going Steady' album,

https://www.uticaod.com/story/entertainment/2021/01/21/darryl-rahn-host-live-performance-promote-new-album/4177371001/

[li] How Dawes' Taylor Goldsmith is Staying Optimistic, https://www.rollingstone.com/music/music-features/dawes-taylor-goldsmith-interview-1092859/

[lii] BJ Barham https://www.rollingstone.com/music/music-country/how-bj-barham-makes-sense-of-trump-nightmare-on-new-american-aquarium-album-629285/

[liii] Tambourine https://tambourine.bandcamp.com/

[liv] Mountain Swallower https://www.facebook.com/mountainswallower

[lv] Izzy Heltai https://www.izzyheltai.com/

[lvi] Liza Anne https://www.nashvillescene.com/music/features/liza-anne-focuses-on-emotional-well-being-on-i-bad-vacation-i/article_a29093b2-9d58-5329-bd60-fe475f266635.html

[lvii] Willy Mason https://www.willymasonmusic.com/

[lviii] Willy Mason https://www.nme.com/features/music-interviews/willy-mason-new-album-already-dead-postcast-out-here-3009859

[lix] Grumpy https://www.charlotteobserver.com/entertainment/music-news-reviews/article243440311.html

[lx] Hotel Fiction https://hotelfiction.com/

[lxi] Hotel Fiction https://www.redandblack.com/culture/dynamic-duo-the-musicians-behind-hotel-fiction/article_90cf450c-3802-11ea-9bff-1b00ec130bbb.html

[lxii] Everlasting Light https://everlastinglightqc.bandcamp.com/

[lxiii] Everlasting Light https://www.rcreader.com/music/everlasting-light-split-with-changeling

[lxiv] The Central https://thecentral.bandcamp.com/

[lxv] Elizabeth Moen https://elizabethmoen.com/

[lxvi] Elizabeth Moen https://www.chicagotribune.com/entertainment/music/ct-ent-elizabeth-moen-chicago-concert-20220409-qzkmurq2lvg7bgrmr4r3stteye-story.html

[lxvii] 1945 https://www.menemshafilms.com/1945

[lxviii] Charlotte (animation film), https://ajff.org/film/charlotte

[lxix] Jews of the Wild West,
https://www.jewsofthewildwest.com,
https://www.ajff.org/film/jews-wild-west
[lxx] The Auschwitz Report
https://www.imdb.com/title/tt9415108/plotsummary?ref_=tt_o
v_pl
[lxxi] Farther, Faster, Together, https://www.artplaceamerica.org
[lxxii] Farther, Faster, Together, https://www.artplaceamerica.org
[lxxiii] Ontario Study Shows Arts and Culture Attract Top Talent,
https://musiccanada.com/news/ontario-study-shows-arts-and-
culture-attract-top-talent/

Lightning Source UK Ltd.
Milton Keynes UK
UKHW012005230123
415851UK00001B/5